J.S. FREE

Order your autographed copy of any of Jihad's books at a 30% discount at www.jihadwrites.com And family, please post a review on www.amazon.com and e-mail Jihad at jihadwrites@bellsouth.net

AUTOGRAPH PAGE

To be used exclusively to recognize that special King or Queen for their support.

This is a work of fiction. Any references or similarities to actual events, locales, real people, living or dead are intended to give the novel a sense of reality. Any similarity in other names, characters, places and incidents is entirely coincidental.

Envisions Publishing, LLC P.O. Box 83008
Conyers, GA 30013

ISBN: 978-0-9706102-8-7

First Printing April 2013
Printed in the United States of America

10 9 8 7 6 5 4 3 21

Submit Wholesale Orders to: Envisions Publishing, LLC
Envisions2007@gmail.com P.O. Box 83008
Attn: Shipping Department, Conyers, GA. 30013

J.S. FREE

APPRECIATION PAGE

There are so many wonderful Kings and Queens that helped make Preacherman Blues II a reality, and I may miss a few but please family, chalk it up to my tired and exhausted mind.

First and foremost I wanna thank the creator, without your inspiration and your spirit I would've given up long ago.

I list book clubs first, because there is absolutely no way that I could have brought THE MESSAGE out without your super support. I wanna thank all the wonderful fans and bookclub members that have continued to support me on my writing journey. Queen Monae Eddins, Queen Loray Calhoun and the Women of Distinction bookclub in Columbus, Ohio, thank you so much for pushing all of my work so hard. Queen Monique Smith and the Queens of Dialogue Divas bookclub Atlanta, Lisa Johnson and the Queens of Sisters on the Reading Edge bookclub Oakland, Queen Gloria Withers and Queen Janene Holland of Chapter 21 bookclub Philadelphia, Queen T.C. at R.A.W. Sistahs, Queen Kanika and K.O.M. bookclub Atlanta, Queen Lenda and Mo' betta views bookclub Atlanta, Queen Dr. Wright and the queens of Sisters in the Spirit 2 bookclub, Queen Tiffany and the Queens of Distinguished Ladies and Gents bookclub Memphis, Queen Wanda Fields, Queen Alethea Hardin and the Queens of Shared Thoughts bookclub New Jersey, Queen Ella Curry of EDC creations, Queen Ellen and the Queens of Reading is What We Do bookclub Newport News, The Queens and Kings of Sugar and Spice book club, NYC,

I know I've missed several Book clubs so please ad your name here. ________________________________

My closest friends, thanks for putting up with me. Queen Victoria Christopher Murray, Queen Reshonda Tate Bilingsley, Queen Tiffany Colvin, Queen Jamise L. Dames, Queen Pamela Hunter. King Travis Hunter, King Rodney Daniel, King Hasaan Morrow, King Corey Mitchell, King Woody Jenkins, King Kevin Elliott, King Kwan, King Maurice Gant, King Wayne Hunter, and King Theodore Palmer.

Thanks to my family for their continued support, my son Prince Xyon Uhuru, Mom, Queen Arthine Frazier, Brother King Andre Frazier, Brother King Michael Wharton and family, Sisters Queen Las-Shl Frazier, and Queen Karen Wharton, Nieces, Gu-Queitz, Luscious, Sadequa, Shami, Baby, Lameeka, and Ronni, Nephews, I-Keitz, D'Andre, and Billy.

SUPERFANS

Queen Ann Joiner of Norfolk thank you. Queen Kariymah of Philly thank you. Queen Tazzy Fletcher thank you. Queen Iliene Butler, New York thank you. Queen Martha and the queens of IPS transportation Indianapolis.

And I give a very special thanks to the Kings and Queens living behind America's prison walls. Without your letters and support, I would have quit long ago. And I may not respond to all letters, but just know that I read every one of them.

THEY SAY BLACK MEN DON'T READ. FOR ALL THE KINGS ON THE INSIDE AND OUTSIDE KEEP PROVING THAT MYTH WRONG.

By supporting my books, you help our young Brothers and sisters realize the kings and queens that they are.

And I'd like to give a very special thanks to President Barack Obama. If a man with the name of Barack Hussein Obama can get past the hate so can a man with the name Jihad Shaheed Uhuru. Please don't judge me by what you think my name means, judge me by my actions and by my character.

Please log onto www.jihadwrites.com to find more about Jihad or to purchase any of his books 30% less than the store price, and if you purchase 3 books anytime on www.jihadwrites.com you get the 4th book absolutely FREE. Please tell others what you think by posting a review on www.amazon.com. Log on to www.jihadwrites.com to sign Jihad's guestbook.

Forever

J.S. Free

Also By Jihad/J.S. Free

Fiction

STREET LIFE
BABY GIRL
RHYTHM & BLUES
MVP
PREACHERMAN BLUES
WILD CHERRY
PREACHERMAN BLUES II
MVP RELOADED
WORLD WAR GANGSTER

Self Help

THE MESSAGE: 16 Life Lessons for THE Hip Hop Generation

Anthology

Gigolos Get Lonely Too
The Soul of a Man

Please pick up any of Jihad's books at your local bookstore or you can save 30% and order Jihad's books from the secured site at **jihadwrites.com** If you purchase 3 books the **4th** is absolutely FREE. Please allow -7 to 10 days for shipping.

SPECIAL MESSAGE FROM J.S. FREE

One of the best kept secrets in the African-American literary industry is the independent author. We are told by you that our books are great and we should get them into all stores. The author can not do that. You, the reader, must ask the stores to carry our books. Most of us are not with the major publishers. Most of the African-American authors are independent publishers or self-published, and do not have the marketing dollars to get in all of the Barnes and Nobles and Borders bookstores. Not to mention, Walmart is virtually impossible for an independent publisher to get into. Now in Urban communities, myself and many independent authors are carried in the mainstream stores, however, many are not. It is you who can get us there by just making a phone call to the store manager requesting that our books are carried. There are several great writers you've never heard of because they are independent, and not enough of us are demanding that they be in stores.

Most important to anyone's success is support, and the best way to show support for any independent author is to help them maximize their sells so they can continue to write. Writing, good writing, is time consuming and very expensive. We love what we do, but we still have to pay bills like everyone else. So please help us continue to do what we love and what you love.

Thank you so much for reading and supporting family.
www.jihadwrites.com

Forever

J.S. Free

THE MESSAGE

16 life lessons for the Hip Hop Generation

A part of our culture should
be the successful transition
from boyhood to manhood.
I sincerely believe it takes a
man to develop boys into men

-Jawanza Kunjufu

TABLE OF CONTENTS

	Why I write	**(3)**
	Letter to my Mother	**(7)**
	Letter to my Son	**(10)**
I.	***Saggin' & Baggin'***	***(12)***
II.	***What Up, Dog?***	***(21)***
III.	***Blaze One***	***(30)***
IV.	***Getting Some***	***(41)***
V.	***A Mind is a Terrible Thing to Waste***	***(56)***
VI.	***A Slave Mentality***	***(68)***
VII.	***I Brought You in This World, I'll Take You Out***	***(80)***
VIII.	***City of Bling***	***(95)***
IX.	***Chocolate M&M's***	***(107)***
X.	***Conversation with a Black Man***	***(116)***
XI.	***The Legend of Bo Jack Jones***	***(133)***
XII.	***Snitch Politics***	***(139)***
XIII.	***Definition of a Gangsta***	***(147)***
XIV.	***Sins of the Father***	***(159)***
XV.	***I pledge Allegiance***	***(171)***
XVI.	***Free Your Mind***	***(175)***

THE MESSAGE

INTRODUCTION

WHY I WRITE

On April 13th 1999, I was released from federal prison after serving over 7 years. My crime – ignorance. My conviction – multiple kilos of cocaine. I was a dope, that happened to sell dope. This, a very popular profession among our young men and women today.

It was in prison that I came into contact with the most inspirational, intelligent, strong men I'd ever met or read about. And, the real tripped out thing about these men was that they looked like me and sounded like me. Although they should have, none of them had an ***S*** on their chests. But, they were and are so much more then SUPERMEN. They were kinky-haired, big lipped, different shades of brown men who had lived a similar life that I had. Unfortunately, their stories would never be told unless I told them, which I have in all of my 12 novels. You see, most of these men will never teach in a classroom, they will never even touch the light of day, and they and you are the reason I write today.

For twenty-two years, twenty-two years, I was a rebel without a cause, a revolutionary without a revolution. No one could tell me anything back then, because I knew everything. I ran through women, sold drugs, partied and committed all kinds of negative acts against people who looked like me – all for the almighty dollar and a few seconds of fame.

A couple years into my prison bid, I began reading and eventually understood what many of the inmates I looked up to had been saying. "I had Bed Time." That meant, before I knew it, I'd wake up, and it would be time for me to go home. They were right, but I didn't come home alone. I came home with THEM, and the ANCESTORS that put gangsta down before the word was even a word.

You see, I always thought I was gangsta, until I read the likes of Dr. Ben, Dr. Na'im Akbar, George Jackson, Geronimo Pratt, Martin Delaney, Malcom X, Marcus Garvey and so many more. Now these KINGS were truly gangsta.

I will never forget Arthur Strong asking me if I could have pulled a trigger and killed another man while I was paralyzed from the waist down. I had said yes, I could have. Then he told me that Robert Beck, better known as Iceberg Slim had only a second or third grade education, yet he manipulated the minds of women, got them to sell their bodies and bring him the money they received. And then he asked me, if I thought that was gangsta. I said something like 24 carrot, USDA gangsta. Then he had me read Visions for Black Men, by Dr. Na'im Akbar. It took months before I actually read it, but when I did, I was in AWE. Strong then told me that anyone can pull a trigger on another black man, anyone can manipulate the minds of women for their own selfish greed, but men like Dr. Na'im Akbar... Men that stand up to a system designed and implemented to destroy the black male before he's even a twinkle in his daddy's eye… Men that fight to the death with no more than an ink pen… Men that refuse to bend and bow, when everyone is going along to get along.

After listening to the Martin's, Malcoms and Marcus's on the inside and reading works from the revolutionary brotha's and so many more that I stated above, I decided that for the rest of my life I would carry the torch and represent gangsta to the fullest. Now that I had been freed from the shackles of my own ignorance, I had to go back and be a Moses for my brothers and sisters that were suffering from their own ignorance that has been given to them by society's social constructs.

I decided to write. Not the shoot-em up, sell some dope, trick off with our sista's, baby momma drama fiction. I decided to write self-help reality fiction books – about the hood – books that show our sista's and brotha's how to rise from their socially constructed hood mentality to their natural former king and queen mentalities.

I speak to our young urban Kings as I have never spoken before in **THE MESSAGE**. *I am so tired of hearing that Black men don't read, and the easiest way to keep a secret from a Black man is to put it in a book.* There are over two million Black and Latino men in prison that will tell you different. And there are even more on the streets who would read if they knew of stories that they could relate to and see themselves in. I write those stories as so may others also do, but we don't get press because we are writing to save instead of enslave.

Through my books STREET LIFE, BABYGIRL, RHYTHM & BLUES, PREACHERMAN BLUES, WILD CHERRY, PREACHERMAN BLUES II, MVP, MVP RELOADED, **THE MESSAGE**, AND WORLD WAR GANGSTER, I edu-tain.

J. S. FREE

I do not write for the Purpose Driven Life readers, I write to the people with purpose but just don't know what it is. I don't write to the Chicken Soup for the Soul readers, I write to the Butter beans for the Soul People.

When I first released this book as The Survival Bible: 16 Life lessons for the young Black Male in 2009, I received over 44 newspaper write ups, the month before it's release. I attempted to get the books in schools and I tried my best to get into schools to do readings and vibe sessions with the students. I failed. I was told that the books title The Survival Bible was inappropriate. I was also scheduled to do an interview with a major news network but it was nixed because my name, Jihad and the word Bible on the book was too controversial. So, now I after four years, I decided to repackage the book because I know without a doubt, that THE MESSAGE has to be read. Please family, help me to make this a reality. These young men and young women are tomorrow. We have a chance to rekindle the spirit of Malcolm, Martin, Marcus, Espanata, Guerva, Tubman, Assata, Winnie, and so many more. Help me re-educate the Urban nation, so we can all one day be free.

Forever,

J.S. Free

THE MESSAGE

Letter to my Mother

I can't imagine what it's like to be a black woman. I can't imagine what it's like to be a single mother, raising three sons. And I dang sure can't fathom what it was like trying to raise a son like me.

I know I gave you grief. I still remember all the times you prayed for me, and ultimately said, "I'm just turning you over to God." Between all the schools I was suspended and expelled from, the many times you came to bail me out of trouble with the law, and all the hospital visits, where you didn't know if I was going to live or die, between all that, you still stood strong. You fussed. You cursed. You went up side my head, but you never turned your back on me. When the doctors told you I would never walk again, you never gave up hope. You thought I was asleep, but I wasn't when you prayed by my bedside as I fought for my life in Intensive care after fracturing two bones in my neck.

I remember when I was a kid, every time I got into trouble, you'd always say I was trying to kill you, that I was trying to give you a heart attack. I really wasn't. I don't know who I'd be or where I'd be if you really would have had a stroke. But thank God you didn't.

When I was in prison, you begged me to keep my mouth closed. I think you knew the guards and administration were doing more than sending me into disciplinary segregation (The Hole) for months at a time, and shipping me from one prison to another. You knew that they were exacting their own form of punishment. It seems the more they beat me, the more they tried to make me look bad amongst the inmates, the louder I hollered injustice and freedom cries. The more I continued to try and enlighten and re-educate anyone who would listen as I spoke of freedom, and revolution of thought, as I was learning and reading the works of pre-eminent African and African-American scholars, you were still concerned about me and just wanted me to do my time, stay safe and get out.

But as you well know, mom, I couldn't shut up then and I can't shut up now, especially when I see or hear about someone enslaved by what they don't know or understand. That's why I write. My pen is my sword. As you once said when I was maybe four or five, *I have the gift of gab*. It's with that gift that I began to fight once I began reading and learning about my culture and finding out who I was. I had to figure out a way to share the love of knowing with others, even if it meant that I would be beat, or worse, killed. There is no way I could lay down, after I found freedom through the pages of books written for the upliftment of our mighty race.

For so long, I robbed, stole, and sold drugs. For so long, I was filled with self-hate and didn't even know it, until

THE MESSAGE

I discovered who I was, thanks to some of the most intelligent men who happened to look like me. Black men who many will never have the privilege to meet because most of those men will never see the light of day from behind America's penitentiary walls. Mom, I make no excuses for the wrong I did or the wrong some of my brothers did. We know the 'whys' (both justified and unjustified) of why I ended up behind bars. But the belief that you can be reborn, that you can stop being a victim and be a *victor,* is real.

For all those who can't be heard. I am their voice. I am the voice of ancestors that most of us don't even know about. I am the voice of freedom, the voice of my mentors that put pen to paper, writing books in hopes of enlightening and freeing the minds of our people, and eventually all people.

This drive, this vision, this voice - all came from God, who passed it down through you and my earthly father. You did the best you could, a fantastic job of raising me. It was God who let me see and live through so much hell so I could appreciate the Heaven I see in you and every enlightened brother and sister I encounter. Thank you, Mom. I love you, appreciate you, and hope that I have done something to make you proud. It is my hope that this book while help at least one other misguided young man from putting his mother through the hell in which I put you. In the pages of this book are true to life essays that I hope will educate and inspire our young black men to aspire to be the Kings that they were destined to be.

I love you mom,

J S Free

J. S. FREE

Letter to my Son

I know it hasn't been as easy as it appears for you, but so much can be attributed to your positive attitude about life. It is not that difficult to survive, rather it is the choices we make to achieve a higher quality of survival.

I give you one example. Your tenth grade school year - a few months after your father passed away - you were expelled form two entire school systems for that whole year. Faced with the distinct probability of leaving your education behind at that point, you researched and found a school that would accept you as you were. I know without a doubt this choice was the best thing that ever happened to you. You desired a higher quality of survival, and St. Luke Area Three Learning Center, housed in a beat-up dilapidated small building above a homeless shelter and filled with unorthodox teachers and students that were outcasts from society, supplied that need.

guidance. Write on son. Write on.

Love you,
Mom

Chapter I

Saggin' & Baggin'

Black men born in the U.S. fortunate enough to live past the age of eighteen are systematically conditioned to accept the inevitability of prison. For most of us, it simply looms as the next phase in a sequence of humiliation.

George Jackson

***"What's the deal, cornmeal*?"** Mark asked as he greeted his best friend, Jermaine at the gate in front of Jermaine's parents' front yard.

"Saggin' & Baggin', baby. You know how I do," Jermaine said, giving Mark a pound.

"I know we gon' miss the school bus if you don't hurry your butt up," Mark said.

"Bump that. I ain't tryin' to get detention for being late," Jermaine said letting his pants fall to his ankles, so he could secure his backpack on his shoulders.

"You advertisin', I'm buyin'." A muscular but short, clean shaven man said as he walked up on the boys. The man dressed in beige Dickies and a matching shirt, nodded. "How much?"

Jermaine frowned. “Who is you?” he asked pulling his pants back up to his thighs.

The man held a finger in the air. “It’s who *are* you, and Interested, is who I am,” the man said as he grabbed his crotch and stared at the skinny sixteen year old.

“No disrespect, but we don’t know you, partna,” Mark said.

“Speak when you spoken to, boy,” the big man said in a commanding deep voice as he pointed a dark ashy finger at Mark.

Mark sized the man up. *Five-eight, five-nine, a muscle head.* The man looked like he played on some NFL football team’s frontline, and he was darker than the color black.

Mark was five-eight, and that was with his Timberland boots. Maybe a hundred thirty pounds and that’s with a wet brick in each pocket. Jermaine was two inches taller at most, but skinny as a rail, something most people couldn’t tell just by looking at him. That’s because Jermaine wore three pairs of boxers, red, white, and blue, under the huge 42 inch waist jeans that were saggin’ right above his knees.

“Cat gotcha tongue, youngin’?” the man asked, staring at Jermaine.

He was making Jermaine nervous. “Man, we gotta jet, before we miss the bus. Come on, Mark.”

“Walk away from me and I’m gon’ take what I want,” the man said. “And I wish you would try to run in them jeans hangin’ under your butt,” the man said with slow calm. His face was a mask of intent sincerity.

“Man, what you want?” Jermaine said, shaking his head from side to side.

“I want what you offerin’.”

For the fifth time in the last few minutes, Jermaine pulled up his pants. "Man, I don't know what you thinkin' but I ain't no punk."

"Really now?" the man asked.

"Man, I don't want no trouble. I'm just tryin' to get to school," Jermaine said, looking around, hoping a neighbor would come outside.

Mark stood next to his friend shivering as the winter wind whipped through the April spring air. His huge T-shirt was waving like a flag.

"That makes both of us. Just got out the joint yesterday. Did a quarter for manslaughter. I stay down the street, out here getting' my walk on, and I sees you and li'l homie hangin' low, and when you let them jeans fall, I knew what it was."

Jermaine waved an arm in the air, "Nah, partna', you…you…you, got the wrong idea. I don't swing like that."

"I can't tell." The strange man licked his lips. The boys looked on as the man cracked his ashy knuckles and flexed his chest muscles. "First, you gon', miss your bus. Second, try to run, I'm gon' catch one of you and you don't even wanna know what I'm gon' do when I catch you. And third, you stand here and listen, while I put you down on some real boss game."

The boys looked at each other. They didn't know what to do or what to think, but they both knew that trying to run would be wasn't the answer.

Oblivious to the wind, and the few cars that passed in front of Jermaine's house, the strange man put a beige timberland-booted foot on the yellow fire hydrant he stood next to. "Back in '84, 1984, I was around y'all age. It was a Friday night, everybody that was anybody hung out at Charle's Disco on Simpson Road. It was a twenty–one and older spot, but back then, it wasn't nothin' to go to Wong Li's Beauty supply, downtown at five points and get a fake picture I.D." He nodded. "Yeah youngin', on Friday's, Charle's Disco was ghetto fab, all the baddest young stunna's and wannabe strippers were on the scene half-butt naked, fishin' for a balla, and a new babydaddy. Me, hell, I was green as grass, but you couldn't tell me and the young stud I rolled with. My dude, Pork chop, was gettin' a little paper slingin' rock for some baby balla dude from the Westside. Matter of fact, Pork chops' boss, let him push his cherry-red I-Roc camaro Z-28 that night."

"Come on, Man. We gon' be mad late to school," Mark said, hoping the ex-con would let them go.

The man shot Mark a look that sent chills up his spine. "Interrupt me one more time," he threatened.

Mark pulled up his pants, and held them up with both hands in his pockets.

"Where was I?" The man looked off into space a moment before snapping a finger. "Oh yeah. So we bobbin' our heads, 'bout to bend the corner on Simpson Road, LL Cool J's first hit *I need a Beat*, blasted from the four 15 inch woofers takin' up the hatch and the back seat, when One-time came outta nowhere and pulled us over."

"'Officer, what did I do?' Pork chop had asked, while letting the driver's side window down."

"'License and insurance,' the office had barked."

"'You was born Black, my dude, that's what you did,' I had muttered a little too loud."

"'Officer needs assistance; I'm at Simpson and MLK. Officer needs assistance, over,' the cop said as he took wide steps around the front of the car with his hand on his gun."

"'Get out,' the officer barked."

"I rolled the window down. 'Huh?' I asked."

"'Get out of the vehicle. Now!' the cop shouted, his hand on his gun."

"I opened the door and began getting out when the cop, grabbed a handful of my hair and pulled me onto the ground, face first."

"'Jheri curl wearing jungle bunny," the cop quipped as he kicked me in the side. 'Hands behind your back, smart guy.' He bent my arms back and slapped handcuffs on my wrist as another squad car pulled up."

"I wanted to scream from the pain in my side, but I was too angry."

"'What's up, Rambo?' I'd heard another cop, a brotha, ask."

"*Thank God*, I remembered thinking. I just knew a brotha would set this Gestapo racist cop straight."

"Both cops roughly pulled me up off the pavement. 'Bruh, we wasn't doing nothin'.' I began addressing the black cop. 'This dude pulls us over for no reason, and comes around the car and assaults me. And he called me a Jheri curl jungle bunny, before kicking me in the ribs.'"

"The black cop looked at the other cop and then back at me. 'You do have a Jheri curl, and if he says you're a jungle bunny,' the cop shrugged, 'then I guess you are.'"

"I turned and looked back inside the car. My dude, was sitting there, hands on the wheel looking straight ahead. I couldn't believe what this sell-out blue, had just said. His words hurt more than the kick in the side from the redneck cop."

"'Did you check for ID?' the black cop had asked, while going through my pockets. 'Jack Johnson, huh?' the black cop read out loud as he looked at my fake ID, with the fake name and date of birth."

"Bruh, did you just hear yourself? The cracka' called me a jungle bunny," I said.

"'My name is Officer Jennings, clown,' the white cop said, before slapping me hard upside my head."

"Without thinking I turned and spit in his face. Next thing I knew the black cop hit me in the back, and I was back on the ground near the curb, getting beat with a flashlight and a nightstick by both cops."

He shook his head sadly. "A couple of hours later I was in the Fulton County jail, battered, bruised, and booked under a fake name. I was scared as you know what, but I was even more angry than I was scared. I was charged with assaulting an officer. Can you believe that, li'l homies?"

Jermaine shrugged his shoulders and Mark just shook his head.

The con continued. "Never having been locked up, I didn't know what to expect. It was a small holding cell, with two other guys inside, a brotha somewhere between, I'd say 25 and 35, and a Hell's Angel-looking long-haired skinny white guy. The cell was a dull paint chipped gray. The rotten pissy smelling holding tank stank so bad I was almost scared to sit down. So, I went and stood in a corner. My back was to the concrete wall. One arm was folded across my stomach while my right hand was cuffed over my nose. I couldn't call my mother. It was past three in the morning. I'd left my eleven-year-old brother home alone, and if I called her at work from jail, she'd know I left him home alone and she would've done much worse to me than the cops and the prison could ever do. I couldn't think of anyone to call, when and if I did get a phone call."

"What about your dad?" Mark asked, like he was suddenly interested in the story.

The con shook his head. "Never met the man."

"What happened next?" Jermaine asked, still holding his pants up.

The con blinked back a tear. "This happened." He pointed at Jermaine. "Same way I came at you young buck, was the exact same way the black dude in the cell came at me."

"Back in the '80's all the young studs wore skin tight jeans, belts, with big shiny silver or gold cowboy-looking buckles, and tight, shiny silk colorful dress shirts. Needless to say, when I was arrested I was clean as the board of health or so I thought. I was a 31 waist, wearing 28 inch Black Jordache jeans and a tight canary yellow button down silk dress shirt."

"I was lost in thought, mindin' my own. I didn't even see the black dude until he was up in my face. He grabbed my butt with both hands and licked my ear." With watery eyes, the con put his hands over his eyes, took a deep breath and continued, "The mother…" he took a breath, closed and opened his eyes. "The man stuck his tongue in my ear. I lost it. I was small, not too much bigger than you homies. Dude was maybe fifty pounds bigger than me. I screamed and just went haywire swinging and pushing the man back. He lost his balance and fell, banging his head on the cell's metal toilet rim so hard he lost consciousness. Still, I continued beating the man. I stomped him in the head and face until the Hell's Angel-looking guy, grabbed me from behind. I slung him off and started beating him unconscious, too. By the time the sheriff's deputies got the cell open, one man was dead, and one was in critical condition."

"My charge was upgraded to murder, and a week later, it became double murder, when the black guy died. My mother didn't have any money for an attorney so I had a public *pretender.* I went to trial, and was sentenced to forty years. I served 25. Why? Because I was trying to be like everybody else, stylin' and profilin', doing the In thing, wearing skintight, uncomfortable jeans, looking like a fool. And young buck, I done seen fads and styles come and go, but the dumbest one," he pointed to Jermaine's knock-off Red Monkey jeans, "is those saggin' pants. In the penitentiary, that was one surefire way to tell who's catching."

"Catching?" Mark asked.

"Yeah, who's takin' pipe. You know, who's advertising their same sex way of life. I just want you li'l homies to think about everything I said. I want you to think about what you wearing, and why you wearing it, and think about how you wearing it, because those are the first impressions anyone gets before you even open your mouths, and that first impression is everything. Before you know it you'll be responsible for yourselves. You'll be wanting jobs, and you'll be hard pressed to get a job looking like you can't even look presentable. It's so much more than that, but I just want you to think li'l homies, don't be me. While you two are walking to school holding your pants up, just think of as many positive things that can come out of you wearing saggin' and baggin' clothes, and then see how many negative things can come from you wearing saggin' and baggin' clothes. Just think, li'l homies. THINK…"

The con walked off, leaving Mark and Jermaine to ponder his words.

For more on sagging go to: ***associatedcontent.com/.../sagging_pants****_hip_hop_trend_or_prison.html*

SELF-REFLECTION

1. Ask yourself: What do you think others see when they see young men wearing clothes three and four times too big, when they have their pants sagging to the knees?

2. Did you know that clothing fads such as wearing plain colored Dickies matching shirts and pants sets come from prison? Dickies are prison-issued clothes with a name tag on them. So, next time you put on a set of beige or green Dickie-like work clothes, think about the two million plus men that have no choice but to wear these same plain clothes every day for years as they serve time behind prison walls. Wearing the prison uniform is just another way of psychologically preparing you for the prison gates.

3. Go inside your urban Burger King and McDonald's restaurants anywhere in America and you can find young men and even young women wearing sagging pants, while flipping burgers, and mopping floors. I've yet to see a fortune 500 executive, a doctor or nurse, an attorney, or a political leader, wearing sagging pants. Do you have a McDonald's fry cook mentality?

4. Are you a follower or a leader? If you think you are a leader, then explain what makes you a leader.

5. If given the opportunity to meet President Obama, would you wear sagging clothes?

THE MESSAGE

Chapter II

What Up, Dog?

Children have never been very good at listening to their elders, but they have never failed to imitate them.

-James Baldwin

June 12, 1859 Norfolk Virginia

"Before we get started, I need everybody to bow their heads," Big Jim said as he looked out at the anxious crowd of men, women, and children. "Dear God, I wanna thank you for bringing us all together on this beautiful sunny day. I wanna thank you for your graciousness in allowing the good God fearin' white men and women folk of Virginia," he paused, extending an arm behind him displaying a long line of shackled and chained tired and battered black men and women, "ta continue doing your work, civilizing the savage beasts that stand before you and behind me. Thank you for salvaging 150 of the 290 nigger cargo that we rescued from the savage jungles of the West African continent, Amen." He banged the gavel down on the podium, atop the platform he stood on. "Let the 82nd Suffolk County State Fair and slave auction begin."

Loud and enthusiastic applause rang out from the huge crowd of patrons. Little boys and girls sat on the shoulders of their fathers and older brothers so they could get a good view of the scene unfolding in front of them.

"First, we have this," he pointed to the man that was separated from the others and was shuffled to the front of the stage, "healthy strapping boy. Just look at him. Big black broad shoulders, strong long legs, and big hands and feet. This here boy is a mule. I knows they brains is small, but this here boy got a big enough noggin' to house a little more brain than the otha' nigras. That oughta make him a tad bit easier to train."

The crowd broke out in laughter.

"And he got some good vocal chords. Just listen. Bark," Big Jim shouted at the naked chained and shackled black man to his right. "I said bark." Big Jim hit the battered and chained man in the ear with the three pound wooden gavel. "Moo, meow, open that mouth boy," Big Jim said, holding the gavel over his head, threatening to take another swing.

The shackled man didn't utter a sound. He just held his head high, and looked out at the crowd as if he were royalty about to address his constituents.

"Two lashes," Big Jim said to the whip bearer.

"One," the crowd counted aloud with Big Jim as the whip bearer lashed the slave's bare back.

Still the proud naked, chained man didn't utter a word. He only made a grunting sound.

Nineteen minutes and twenty lashes later, the man barked, mooed, and meowed.

"Looka here, you see what a little discipline can do. In less than a half hour, I done taught the boy how to sound like three different animals. Now don't worry 'bout all the blood and the damage to his back. Animals have a natural way in healing up. These nigra animals is not quite near as smart as a housecat, but they is definitely loyal as dogs as long as you feed 'em and discipline them. Now let's start the bidding.

Two hours later, Bartholomew Washington and his ten-year-old son, Bradley were loading up the beaten slave and a couple others he'd purchased at the state fair auction.

"Dad, why do we need more slaves?" young Bradley asked his father.

"Because son, we can clean em' up, breed 'em like we do our foxhounds, and..."

"Sell their pups off," young Bradley said, interrupting his father.

"Well, yes son, but we can sell the big one's we don't need for more than we bought them for. They work the fields and the slophouses for a year, we make money all around the board. And we can get almost as much for their litter as we can our foxhound litter," Bart said patting his red headed son on the back, before getting inside the horse carriage, with the three slaves strapped behind the buggy.

"Calm down, boy," Bart said to one of the four healthy fox hounds that rode inside the large carriage. "They ain't gon' bite," Bart said to the dog, barking at the slaves that walked behind the carriage.

June 12, 1959 Norfolk Virginia

"Looka here, looka here, looka here. Do you see what I see, Cat daddy?" Mario said addressing his friend as they stood outside the liquor store.

"See it, baby, my eyes is on the sparrow. That foxy momma got my name invisibly written all on her backside," Boo-Boo said right before taking a swig from the brown paper bag.

"Let me hit that," Mario said reaching out for the bottle. After taking a swig from the bottle, Mario walked over to the bus stop where the woman stood. "Say momma, what a fox like you doin' out by yourself this time a'night."

"Excuse me?" She turned.

"A fox like *yourself* need a cat like *myself* to protect you from all the hounds that surely be barkin' up your tree."

"What is your name?" the lady asked.

He took off his brown fedora. "They call me Dog, but you can call me anything and anytime." He smiled.

The city bus's lights could be seen in the distance.

"I didn't ask what they called you. I asked what your name was," she said.

"Ah, foxy momma, it don't matter what my name is. It matter what I…"

"My name is Lenora. I am a woman not an animal, you remember that. Now if you see me again, you either address me as Lenora, Ms., or ma'am."

The bus came to a stop.

"Foxy momma, let me give you a ride." Mario said looking behind him in the direction of his ten-year-old half-running Buick. "My car is parked right over there." By the time he turned his head back toward her, she was getting on the bus.

"Dragon mouth, B&%*ch, you gon' play a player like that. You just gon' ignore a boss cat like myself?"

Lenora turned at the top of the buses stairs. "You still a slave, full of the virus. The worst part is you don't even know it," she said shaking her head before the double rear doors closed.

June 12, 2009 Norfolk, Virginia

"Who's the baddest b&%ch you know, girl?" Lameeka asked Renee.

"Uh, that would be me," Renee said, as the two teens walked through the hall, heading toward the high school cafeteria.

"Not!" Lameeka stuck out her left hand in a stop sign gesture. "No, I am that B&%ch, all young B&%ches should strive to be like. I'm 16, and I rocks Prada, and Versace on a regular. Dooney, and Louey call me on my cell to approve their new lines of purses and," she pointed a gold glitter fingernail in the air, "let me emphasize the *and*," she placed a hand on her hips. "Dudes be fightin' to spend that paper on a B&%ch. In the words of the second baddest B&%ch in the land, Li'l Kim, *'Queen b&%ch, supreme &%tch, kill a nigga for my nigga by any means b&%ch. murder scene b&%ch, clean b&%ch, disease free b&%ch.*' And girl, I be that b&%ch that Li'l Kim rappin' about."

"My Niggettes. What up Dogs?" Trey called out, while catching up to the girls.

"What it do, dog?" Lameeka responded, touching fists with Trey.

"It do what I make it do, Queen Bee," Trey said, as they all walked into the lunch room.

"Nigga, you know you ain't need to summarize my gangsta. Sound my name out. Queen B%#ch, not no Queen Bee," Lameeka said.

"My bad, Queen B%#ch," he said." He turned. "Yo, big dog," he called out to where the lunch line ended. "I'm gon' catch up with you B%#ches later," he said, about to run off.

"Hold on, little buddy," Mr. Chambers, the head of security at MLK High said, putting a hand on Trey's shoulder. "All three of y'all," he addressed the girls and Trey, "come with me," he commanded while, walking out of the cafeteria, the three students behind him, voicing their protests.

Mario Chambers had worked in the school system for forty-nine years. Thirty as a janitor, and for the last nineteen, he'd been a crossing and security guard.

Minutes later, the two young ladies, and Trey sat in front of Mr. Chambers, in his small office.

"What did we do?" Trey asked.

"What you all have is very contagious. The good new is, I have the cure." Mr. Chambers stood up, his belly covered the black security belt around his waist. "I too, was afflicted with the same disease most of us, and you three have."

"Man, I ain't got no disease," Renee blurted out.

"Me neither. Whachu you talkin' about?" Lameeka asked sucking her teeth.

"Oh, you got it." He shook his head. "You all got it bad, and if you're not cured, the chances of you having a good life are extremely slim."

"Man, what are you talking about?" Trey asked.

Mario Chambers was one of the coolest old heads that worked at MLK High. He always kept it real, and shot straight with everybody. He'd tell you what was on his mind if you wanted to hear it or not.

"Back in slavery times, the slave master infected us with the virus. He beat our ancestors until they gave up their names and took on the one's he wanted us to have. Names that separated us from our families, tribes, culture, our history. And after a couple generations, we had all but forgotten who we were. We were beaten into accepting our condition."

"Come on man, how many times we done heard that same ol' song?" Trey asked.

"You may have heard the song, but you need to listen to the lyrics. Now the sooner you let me finish, the sooner you can get back to being ignorant," Mr. Chambers said. "As I was saying, before we were kidnapped from our homes and brought to these shores, we were proud people. We knew who we were, and where we were going."

Trey tapped Lameeka on the knee, before looking back up at Mr. Chambers. "If we knew where we were going, how did we end up as slaves in America?" Trey asked.

"Drugs and alcohol. That's how. The slave master could only master the slave by making someone a slave. What is a slave? A slave is anyone who mentally submits themselves to another. Give someone drugs and or alcohol and they become high. Not in control of themselves. Easily manipulated by others who *are* in control of *themselves,* therefore enslaving them. The number one drug of the slave master is deception. And after being deceived for generations, we have become the deceivers."

"I'm confused," Renee said.

"Yeah, me too," Trey said twisting his neck.

"Okay, call a man a dog for five six generations. I mean every day all day. If he's not strong in knowing who he is, and his foundation, where he came from, then he'll eventually begin to question who and what he is subconsciously. He begins acting like a dog, sniffing behind everything with a skirt, having babies and leaving them to the mother and the state to raise, and a few generations later, no longer does the slave master need to call you a dog. You call yourself and others like you, who don't know who they are, dogs. Using the term endearingly mind you. And worst you act like animals. Many act like mad dogs or dogs in heat.

"When I was your ages, it was cat, cat daddy, cool cat, foxy momma. All animals. A generation later it's dog. My dog, big dog, and the B word. When I was young, call a woman a B and it's time to fight. But we call each other what we do, because we don't realize that we are sick. We don't realize that the Ignorant Virus has plagued a nation of black folks. You ever hear a white man saying what's up cracka', my honkie? You ever hear a white woman bragging on how she is the Queen B?"

Lameeka put a hand over her mouth. "You heard me, Mr. Chambers," she said all bug eyed.

"Didn't need to. I hear enough, and I've heard enough. As easy as it is to say Dog, Cat, B, you can say King, What's up, Queen, because then you are talking about the essence of who you are and who you came from. Try it. Start calling your friends King and Queen, and we can start a happy, positive, feel good revolution.

THE MESSAGE

SELF-REFLECTION

1. Why would you call yourself and your friends by animal names?

2. Why are blacks the only race that addresses each other using animal names?

3. What difference does it make how you address someone?

4. You whistle at dogs. You whistle at women. You call women names that are worse than what you call your household pet. Those same whistles and names someone has called your mother, grandmother, sister, aunt, girlfriend, wife. How does that make you feel?

5. What did you learn from this story?

Chapter III

Blaze One

The tragedy in life doesn't lie in not reaching your goals. The tragedy lies in having no goals to reach.

-Benjamin E. Mays

"Young Dro', wait up," JT hollered out as he jumped off the porch and ran to catch up with his friend, Andro.

"Shawty?" JT said catching his breath. "What it do?"

"It do what I make it do," Andro said giving the much older JT a pound. "On my way to school."

"What 'dat be 'bout?" JT said frowning up. "You been on some ole SpongeBob Square Pants lame kick these last couple weeks."

"Nah, man, I'm still Dro'. I just gotta handle my business."

"What bizness? Yo." JT bobbed his head. "Peep game." He pulled a clear, rolled up baggie out the pocket of his sagging Dickie work pants. "Smell this." He put the baggie to Dro's nose.

"Smell a'ight," Andro said.

"A'ight." He frowned up." Cuz, this some Osama Bin Laden, certified Pakistani Indo. Man, this doe' will make you strap a bomb on ya back, wit' a happy face plastered across your mug." JT playfully slapped Andro on his back. "Come on, Dro', skip school, blow some trees wit' your boy. And after we get right we can catch the Marta down to the welfare office and pick up a couple food stamp freaks."

Andro stopped at the corner. He could see his high school where they stood. It was still about a four block walk.

"Look JT, I'm seventeen in the eleventh grade with tenth grade credits. I'm already a year and a half behind, my GPA is non-existent, and I'm always forgettin' stuff. Simple stuff. I'm squarin' up, dude. I gotta prepare for my future, 'fore I won't have one."

"Squarin' up! Future!" JT patted his chest, "Cuz, this me. Your boy." He held up the bag of weed. "This is the future. Get high til' we die. Smoke 'til' we choke. And sell what we can't smoke."

Andro knew JT wouldn't understand. He'd avoided him for over a week now. He knew this day was coming, but he hadn't prepared a script to convince JT that he was changing his life.

"Cuz, you know my moms be home all day sweatin' me about a J.O.B. You got the crib to yourself until six." JT crossed one arm over his stomach and rested one hand under his chin. "Tell you what, skip school today, let's get blazed, and pick up a couple lonely welfare mommas down at social services, and at the end of the day if you still feel the same way, I'll respect your groove, cool?"

Andro conceded, giving JT some dap. They turned and began walking back toward the house that Andro shared with his mom, and now his Uncle Keitz. Andro couldn't tell

JT his real motivation for conceding to JT. So he decided to show him.

Fifteen minutes later, the two walked into the kitchen through the side door.

"You forgot something?" Keitz asked without turning around. His back was to JT and his nephew. Keitz wore some prison-issued beige shower shoes, a pair of white boxers and a matching wife beater T-shirt. "I would offer you and your company some breakfast, but this is all the eggs we got," he said flipping his veggie omelet over in the skillet.

"Nah, I ain't—"

"Haven't," Keitz corrected.

"Haven't forgotten anything."

Keitz moved the fork to the side and poured the omelet onto a paper plate, before turning around.

"Little, JT," Keitz shouted, staring at JT. "Nah, that ain't you. Can't be. All grown up. Little pissy pants, JT Elliott."

JT stood there wondering who this dude was. He thought about calling him out about the pissy pants comment but the thought quickly passed since this dude looked, and was built like the actor Ving Rhames.

"Me and your brother, Grip was tight. I still think about him." Keitz shook his head.

"My bad, JT," Andro said, looking at a confused looking JT. "This is my Uncle I-Keitz, but we call him Keitz."

Keitz put his plate down on the counter and embraced JT. "You look good, little brotha'. How's Ms. Ann?"

"She's good. She don't work no more, cause of her Sugar, and her High blood-pressure, but she ain't let that slow her down."

Keitz nodded. “Good for her. And you, JT, whachu doing for it?”

He shrugged, “Man you know, with the recession, it’s rough out here. Ain’t no jobs, and if you *do* find somebody that’s hiring, they sho’ nuff ain’t trying to hire a brother with a felony in his jacket.”

“Did you go to college? You gotta trade?” Keitz asked.

“Nah, not really. I just do a little this and that, you know,” JT said.

“A little this and that, huh?” Andro, why you say, you came back home?” Keitz asked.

“I didn’t say Unc. But JT is one of my road dogs—”

“I don’t see no animals in here, do either of you?” Keitz asked.

Both of them shook their heads, wondering why Keitz came out the blue with that question.

“Just wanted to make sure.” He nodded. “I see two men and if I had a mirror I’d see three. JT is a man, Andro, not a road dog. He doesn’t walk on all fours. I don’t wanna hear you call anyone a road dog again, nephew. Now finish telling me why you aren’t in school.”

“JT, got an ounce of Indo weed, and he convinced me to cut school.”

“I thought we-”

“Hold on, Unc.” Andro stuck out his arm before Keitz could go off. “JT is my friend. I’m not going back on anything I committed to, but I brought him here to talk with you.” Andro looked at JT. “Sorry, JT, but my Uncle is the reason I’m squaring up. You need to listen to him. Dude, I love you too much to not try and save you.”

“Save me? Save me from what?”

"From yourself," Keitz said, before turning to his nephew. "I'm proud of you, nephew. Now you go on to school. I got this," he said looking back at JT.

"All right, Unc." JT glanced over at his friend. "You better appreciate this. I'm gon' not only miss first period, but I'm getting detention because of you."

JT stuck his arms out. "Hey, I don't know what type of time you two is on, but I gotta date with some Philly blunts and some doe'. It was good meeting you, big homie, but I'm outta here like last year." He turned to leave.

"Open that door if you wanna swallow every tooth you got in your mouth," Keitz said, his voice filled with force. "Go on to school now, Andro, I said I got it from here."

Andro couldn't get out of the kitchen door fast enough.

"Hold on, pimpin." JT waved an arm in front of Keitz. "You got the wrong one. I'm a grown man. You ain't just gon' talk to me any ol' kinda way."

Keitz took a couple steps forward. A paper plate with eggs and toast separated the two men. "You may be grown in age, but you have child's mentality, so I will speak to you and handle you like you act, and handle yourself."

"Say what?"

"So, now you deaf, huh?"

"Nah, homie, I just wanted to make sure I heard you right."

"Look, fool, you already gon' make me call in. I only been on the job for a week, I might lose it, but it is what it is. I'll get or I'll make another job. I can't get or make another you. Now, what you are going to do is, come into the dining room and sit your narrow behind down in one of my sister's dining room chairs while I eat these cold eggs, and last, you are going to take some of that wolf out your voice. I hope we understand each other." He paused, staring at JT's slim, but tall frame. "Cause if we don't…"

JT knew better than to leave his burner at the crib. But he didn't expect any drama on his block, especially this early in the morning. "Big homie, you don't even know me for real, for real." He shrugged while taking a seat at the dining room table. "Why you all up in mine?"

Keitz swallowed his food, and leaned toward JT. "Cause I can. And, because," he stood up from the table and pointed to his mid section, where a big tattoo covered his whole stomach. "*At war for life*. I had this engraved on me while doing time in Jackson State Penitentiary. My war is against anything and anyone trying to take another young brother's mind off the freedom prize, as mine and so many minds are taken every day, by our mis-educational, one-sided school system, our unjust judicial system, and our mis-guided bass-ackward traditional beliefs."

JT took the baggie from his pocket and began pouring the contents onto the Cherrywood dining room table.

"What are you doing?" Keitz asked, finishing up the last of his omelet.

"I figure I'm gon' be here for a while, might as well put one in the air."

"Put it up or it's going down the sink," Keitz said with a calm seriousness. "Your brother was high. He thought he was smoking some killa weed, but in all actuality, it was laced with Angel Dust. Grip was older than me, but we were close. I knew him well. He didn't touch sherm, acid, or anything stronger than weed. But that night, eighteen years ago, July 4th 1991, we were at a private party on the rooftop of some condo downtown, when Grip started flapping his arms like a bird. He kept saying he was black Superman.

Nobody paid him no mind, 'cause he was always clowning. Before we knew it, he jumped off the thirty-one story building. JT, he was high on," Keitz pointed to the plastic baggie, "weed laced with dust. He's dead. How old are you? Twenty-one, twenty-two?

"Twenty-three," he muttered.

"Same age as Grip when he jumped to his death. You wanna be like Grip? You wanna die at twenty-three? The prime of your life. Or do you wanna be like me, thirty-six years old, living in your sister's basement, after serving half your life behind bars for armed bank robbery? I robbed First National after smoking some sherm, so I could cop some weed and some blow to put out on the streets." Keitz stood up. "Look at me, JT. Just take a look at me. Because I am you in thirteen years, if you don't wake your ignorant behind up."

"Man, I ain't you and I sho ain't my brother. I'm my own man."

Keitz shook his head. "No you're not. You're a ho', and your pimp is the dried leaves in that plastic bag." Keitz pointed to the plastic baggie. "You don't have a job, but you got two, three hundred dollars worth of dope spread out on my sister's dining room table. *A man?* That's what you think you are? Your momma's sick and living off of disability and social security, probably. And your grown behind, living at home, leaching off of her, and running around with a seventeen-year-old kid. Where is the manliness in that? Huh? Answer me, JT!"

JT knocked the dining room chair back, jumping out of his seat. "Ain't no jobs out here. I done tried. Ain't nobody trying to hire a black man with a rap sheet! I tried, man! I tried! I ain't got no skills. All I know is these streets. All I know is slinging dope, hustlin'."

Keitz shook his head. "Nah, you know so much more, but you don't even know what you know, 'cause you can't think right high half the time. But, I will say this, knowing that you don't know is the first step. So what you gon' do about not knowing?"

JT had a look on his face like he really wanted to find a different way. "What can I do?"

"First, you can clear your head. Stop letting drugs cloud your thinking. And don't give me that, smoking herb clears your head foolishness. That's bull. It's a depressant. That means it slows you down. The root of the word is depress, to hold back. You said yourself that we're in a recession; the next worst thing is a *depression.* The media tells you we're in a recession but we are really in a depression. And while the country is recessing and being depressed, you have to press on. It's not like the military went door to door, took everyone's money and credit cards and burnt them in a large oven. There is more money in circulation now than it was in the Clinton era when the economy was stable."

He took a deep breath as he continued. "So I say this to say, that as long as grass grows you got a job. So don't give me mess about nobody hiring. Hire yourself. You got enough money to buy that Indo, you have enough to go on line to Craigslist and buy a used lawnmower, a weed eater, and a rake. You can go door to door for now, and graciously ask your neighbors if you can cut their grass, clean their yards, and what not. You can buy a water hose, some supplies, and go door to door and ask your neighbors if you can wash their cars. You can buy a used pressure washer online and go to small business owners and ask them if you can pressure wash their parking lots. You say you know these streets, all you know is hustlin'. You will be on the streets and you will be hustlin'. But you are only hustlin' backward if you keep spending your money getting high, escaping reality, escaping the real world, like your brother did. Like I did. Like over one-third of our young brothers are doing. So tell me, JT, whachu' gon' do?"

JT put his hands behind his head. "Man, I don't know."

Keitz slapped JT upside his bald head. "What the hell you mean you don't know."

"I don't know!" he shouted.

"You gon' know when you come home one day from doin' nothing and your momma's laid out on the living room floor, dead as a doorknob?" He popped him again. "You gon' know when your momma gets the call that her last and youngest child is found dead, or has been arrested again? You gon' know when your mother dies of a broken heart about her boys? You gon' know when your sons or daughters are found dead in a drug related homicide? You gon' know when your daughter is locked up for selling her body for drugs?" Keitz shouted as he continued slapping JT upside his head.

JT slid to the ground with his back to the dining room wall. "You right." He shook his head. "I can't keep letting my momma down. I don't know how you know, but I have two kids. Justin is two and Simone is four. They don't even live five miles from me and I might have seen them both a dozen times, and I ain't never done anything for them. Nothing. Exactly like my father ain't done nothing for me and Grip. I can't let them down. I don't want them to be like me," he cried.

"You can't let yourself down, JT." Keitz slid to the floor beside JT. "You have to man up." Keitz took JT in his arms and embraced him in a bear hug. "I know you don't know how to be a man. I didn't know how until real men in prison who will never see the freeworld as we see it, taught me what it was to be a man. What it was to take responsibility for myself first and then others."

"Why? Why would you do this? Why would you help me?" JT sniffed, not at all worried about his tough image.

"'Cause I love you, and I love what I know you can be. I'm doing this because I love me. I'm doing this because I love my father and he tells me that I am my brother's keeper. He tells me to do unto others as you would have them do unto you. And as I honor my father, I honor His sons, and His daughters. I honor you, lil' brother and for the sake of your own brother, I hope that you'll honor yourself."

SELF-REFLECTION

1. Why do you think so many young adults smoke marijuana?
2. Do you smoke weed? Have you ever tried it? And how did it or does it make you feel?
3. Name five long term effects of smoking marijuana.
4. Why do you think people like to get high, or if you smoke, why do you get high?
5. Can you relate to anyone in the above story?

Chapter IV

Gettin' Some

What's between your legs doesn't
define you, but the way you use
what's between your ears
definitely does

-Jihad Uhuru

"Soooooo?" Tarik Washington stood, his arms crossed in front of his large frame. His irritation at his friend Miles, written all over his face.

Miles shrugged. "So what?"

The pair were standing in front of the huge oak tree near the school bus stop. Their other best friend, Popcorn stood next to Tarik, just as irritated.

"Come on, man. We both been blowing your phone up all day yesterday," Popcorn said pointing a finger at Miles.

"My fingers are numb from texting your butt," Tarik said. "Why you playin' games? Did you get some or what?"

"Get summa' what?" Miles asked.

Tarik grabbed Miles and pulled him into a headlock.

"I suggest you spill the beans or there gon' be a lotta hymn singin' and flower bringin', and I ain't gon' shed one tear at your funeral, cause you wanna hold back on your boys," Tarik said.

"A'ight, a'ight, let me go before your big behind start thinkin' I'm a Twinkie," Miles said breaking loose from his friend.

"Yo' momma wasn't askin' me to let her go last night," Tarik joked.

"Ohhhh, you wanna talk about my momma now?" Miles said. "That's exactly why I ain't telling you two crack babies nothin'." Miles raked a finger across his lips."My lips are sealed."

It was Monday morning, two days after the junior prom. The boys had a ritual of arriving at the school bus stop extra early on Mondays to discuss the previous week's events. The three had been best friends since elementary school. Popcorn was the coolest of the trio. He had the cutest girls jockeying for his attention. They just loved his curly hair and his hazel brown eyes. Tarik was the athlete, lettering in football in the ninth grade and he was now the best defensive lineman in the state, and he was only a junior. And then there was Miles, the school boy. Straight A's since forever, and the plainest of the trio.

The three rolled on the ground, messing up their school clothes, but Tarik and Popcorn didn't care. Miles was holding out and they weren't getting on anyone's bus until he talked.

"Okay, okay, let me up," Miles said as both Tarik and Popcorn held him down.

"Nope. We can stay here until the day after forever, just like this, until you tell us," Tarik said.

"So, did you get some, or what?" Popcorn asked, holding Miles's legs.

Miles smiled, before nodding.

Tarik and Popcorn got off of him. "Baby boy done finally popped that cherry," Tarik said.

"First we get a black president, next Miles gets his first piece. Next thing you know Black folks will start uniting." Popcorn put a hand on Miles' shoulder and shook his head. "Free at last, free at last, God almighty you's now a man, boy, and you is free at last," Popcorn sang in a southern drawl.

The three made feeble attempts to dust themselves off, but the ground had been moist from all the rain yesterday, so all three of them looked like clothed mud wrestlers.

The boys sat by the big oak, ignoring the long line of high school kids getting on the school bus.

"Okay, tell us what happened. Everything," Popcorn said.

Miles smiled. "Now I know why they call her '*drop it like it's hot, Dreanna'.*" Miles put a hand over his heart. "I think I'm in love."

"Nah, tell me it ain't so. Miles gets his first piece and he voices the forbidden L word. Nah, not Miles," Tarik joked.

"I thinks the boy is whipped." Popcorn said. "Beat down. Body slammed. PW'ed. Thrashed with the poo-nanny, runaway slave-style."

Since they hadn't gotten on the bus, they'd had to walk the ten blocks to school.

"When you two went off in the limo, after the prom, Dreanna asked me to walk her home," Malik continued as they began their journey.

"You a better man than me." Tarik shook his head. "I would'a tripped. We up in a Navigator stretch limo, on our way to get our eat on and your date ready to cut the party short."

Miles had been secretly relieved that Dreanna had wanted to go home early. She'd been putting her tongue in his ear and had been rubbing up against his crotch all evening. He loved his boys to death and he wanted to fit in, but he probably was the only boy at Southwest Dekalb High School who was still a virgin.

He didn't know any boy his age that was still a virgin. Every day, all day his boys and every boy he went around seemed to talk about getting some. The only reason he'd asked Dreanna to the prom was because of Tarik and Popcorn, both had been with Dreanna in the school locker room a few months back. They'd all skipped third period and met in the boy's locker room. Tired of being teased and tired of being the *Last Man Standing* as Tarik and Popcorn had called him, he decided prom night would be his coming out night. His right of passage into manhood. That was before the limo picked him up from Dreanna's house to go to the prom. She was an octopus, her hands and mouth constantly on him.

"Yeah, I wanted to trip, but I didn't. Just walked her home," Miles said.

"I'm confused," Tarik said, shaking his head.

"Can I finish please?"

The boys nodded.

"Well, when we got to her front door, I pulled out my cell to call moms when Dreanna asked me who I was calling. I told her, and she laughed. She told me her mom would take me home. So we went inside, and her mom and some dude was on the couch, dang near in the act themselves. I swear Dreanna's mom looked up from under the dude that was on top of her and waved us away. Dreanna immediately led me up the stairs to her room. That's where the attack happened."

"You are officially da' man," Popcorn said. "So her momma a freak, too?"

Miles shrugged. "Look, I have to come clean." He put his hands in his pockets and stopped walking. "I am scared to death. I didn't use a rubber. I can't have no kids. I can't ask Dreanna to have an abortion. Y'all know I got plans to be an architect, and now I don't know what to do?"

"Quit trippin', Miles. Dreanna probably on the pill, the way she givin' it up, and ain't got no kids. You oughtta be worried about being burnt," Tarik warned.

Miles was worried about that, too. When he woke up and went to pee this morning, a burning sensation almost brought tears to his eyes. But he didn't feel like sharing that with his boys.

"How you gon' go up in her butt naked? You must got a death wish. Dreanna probably got all type of viruses breeding up in her," Tarik said.

"Dude, chill. You see he's serious," Popcorn said.

"I'm serious, too." Tarik countered. "Did you at least smell down there before you hit it, like we told you to?"

"Yeah," Miles said.

"And?"

"I didn't smell no odor and she didn't have no bumps down there," Miles said.

Tarik nodded. "Well then, there you have it. You not burnin', but you still may have crabs."

"Are you itching down there?" Popcorn asked.

"Nah."

"Okay then, you good. You done gone and got you some, and now you trippin'," Popcorn said. "We Veterans, when it comes to gettin' some. Trust, we know when to worry, and as long as it smells clean, and ain't no bumps down there, and she don't have no bumps around her mouth, she clean. Take it from me, Captain Hit It, and," he pointed to Tarik, "my co-pilot, Lieutenant Get Some, we know how to tell if a female got the heebeegeebees."

*****

Miles tried to pull Dreanna away from her girls a couple times during the school day. Each time he looked her way, she avoided eye contact with him. It was as if nothing had happened between the two of them. He sent her a text as soon as school let out asking her if she was on something. She sent him a text back. *That's for me to know and you to find out, daddy. LOL. What kind of childish games was she playing?* he wondered. He would've stepped to her after school if he wasn't so scared - not of her, but of what was going on with his own body. He had held his pee as long as he could both times he went to the bathroom. And both times he had to grit his teeth and bite his tongue to endure the burning sensation he felt after peeing.

He couldn't tell his boys. They'd clown him too hard and he couldn't take it, especially now that his dreams of being an architect seemed like a passing memory. If Dreanna was pregnant then there was no doubt in his mind that he would marry her and get three jobs if he had to, in order to support her and his baby. He didn't even like the girl, but he refused to even entertain the idea of him being like his daddy, whom he'd never met. A few two, three, and four letter acronyms came to mind, as did a few terms. HIV, VD, AIDS, Herpes, and Crabs, but nothing put fear in him like the possibility of him doing to someone what his father had done to his mother. Given her two babies, starting her on a baby-making mission when she herself was just a child.

He sent a text message to his mother. *Mom, I'm on the way to your job. I have a 911.*

Thirty minutes later he walked into the Kentucky Fried Chicken, waved at his mom, Maleka, who was taking an order at the cash register. Miles went and took a seat at a booth. He stared at his mother and was saddened by how hard she worked to provide for him and his four brothers. A tear welled up in his eyes as he thought about not being able to buy his mom a big house and put his siblings through school. For as long as he could remember his mom had worked at least two jobs. She didn't have a life, no boyfriend, nothing, and with her being a diabetic, he just wanted to take care of his mom and never have her want for anything.

She took her scarf and hairnet off. Her long black silky hair dropped onto her shoulders. Miles smiled. He was proud that his mother was the coolest, and prettiest mom in the world. His boys were always cracking jokes on how beautiful his mom was. Miles had no doubt that his mom would have been a super model, movie star, or some type of superstar if it weren't for him and his siblings.

"So, what's up, my young King," Maleka asked, sitting down next to Miles.

"Mom," he shook his head, "I'm so sorry."

"Come on." She stood like she could immediately tell that her son was in distress. "Let's go out here and talk." She led him to the glass doors of the KFC.

"Maleka, I need you at the register. You've already had your break. Now come on," Theresa, the assistant store manager said when she noticed them leaving.

"I have a situation on my hands." Maleka looked at the much younger, heavyset woman. "I'll be back in fifteen minutes."

"I can't promise that you'll have a job in fifteen minutes," Theresa snapped.

This was one of the reasons Miles had to make it big. He couldn't stand how others talked down to his mother. He was only five-foot-seven and toothpick-thin, but still nice looking. He was non-athletic, and no Mr. Personality either, but he possessed a disciplined determination to succeed that was unparalleled among his peers and most adults - and it all stemmed from watching his mother struggle.

Why did that manager have to embarrass his mom in front of customers and the staff? Some of her co-workers attended school with him, so he knew they were just eating it up.

The only reason Maleka wasn't a manger at any of the three fast food restaurants she worked at, was because of all the days she had to take off for her diabetes and tending to her kids.

"Let me tell you something, Theresa." Momma smiled. "I'll always have a job as long as I don't speak to or look down on others like you do. Now, I have to see about my young King, so if this job is gone when I get back," she shrugged, "I'll just get another. Come on, King," Momma said, escorting Miles out of the KFC.

They stood behind the building where he began relaying what was on his mind.

"After the prom, I went to Dreanna's house."

"Miles?" Maleka lifted his chin. "Always hold your head up high when speaking to someone. No matter how you feel. Remember, an act or event can be shameful, but you are a King, and a King must stand proud always, even when they've done something not to be proud of. Now head up and tell me what's wrong."

"I had unprotected sex at Dreanna's house after the prom."

"Where was her mother?"

"Downstairs on the couch with her boyfriend."

"Miles…" Maleka said with deep disappointment lines in her forehead.

"I'm sorry, Mom. I let you down. I tried. I planned to wait. My friends, you know everybody is doing it, and talking about it. I mean all the kids at school. I felt like the last American Virgin."

The May sun was beaming. Beads of sweat danced on Miles and his mother's body, as they stood in back of the KFC next to the dumpster.

"King, oh my beautiful impressionable young king," Maleka said as she rubbed her fingers over her son's short wavy hair. "You can never let me down. As long as you are truthful and you learn from your mistakes, you won't let me or yourself down. Have a seat." She pointed to a cinder block next to the dumpster.

"I got pregnant with you when I was fourteen, and by twenty I had five kids by four different men. And guess what?"

"What?" Miles asked.

"My girls bragged and talked as if they were experienced women, and when I got pregnant, not only did some come clean about still being virgins, but those same girls, one being your aunt Tammy, have gone on to become very successful business women, and wives.

"Now, I don't regret you or any of your brothers, but what I do regret is not having a father to teach me about the love between a woman and a man, from a man's perspective.

Now, I'm not blaming that for my actions, but it is what it is. Maybe I wouldn't have gotten love and sex misconstrued if I had a father. It wasn't until I was pregnant with your youngest brother, that I found out that I was HIV positive."

"Huh?" He stared at her like he must've misunderstood her.

She slowly nodded. "Yes, baby, I'm HIV positive."

Her words slowly registered with him and he began shaking his head. "HIV! Mom! No! No! No!"

She grabbed and hugged her son. "That's when I grew up." She squeezed him tight. "That's when I started reading everything I could on black boys, and black men. That's when I woke up. That's when I vowed to do whatever I had to make sure you boys wouldn't be like me or the men that I had slept with."

"Why didn't you tell me?"

"I didn't want to scare you or your brothers."

"So, you're not diabetic?"

"No, son."

He jumped up from his cement seat. "But, look at you. You are like picture perfect beautiful. You have long hair, you're not super skinny. You don't look like you're HIV positive."

"There is no HIV positive look. Anyone can have AIDS. I don't know what the statistics are now, but five years ago in 2004, 55 percent of all reported HIV cases were among African-Americans. We make up less than 13 percent of the population in this country but 55 percent of all reported HIV cases were among young black Queens and Kings. Sixty-two percent were young black Kings. In 2007, 370,000 kids were infected with HIV. 370,000! Son, 50 percent of all new HIV cases are among young people between the ages of 13 to 24. And the number one target group are black males. In 2000, over nine million young men and women between the ages of 15 and 24 were treated for a sexually transmitted disease. That was nine years ago, I can't imagine what the stats are now."

"I had no idea," Miles said, still stunned. "I wasn't even concerned about HIV. I was more worried about Dreanna being pregnant.

"Is she on birth control?"

"I don't know." He shrugged his shoulders. "She wouldn't tell me."

"What do you think you should do, Miles?"

He stood up and crossed his arms. A minute passed, before he spoke. "First, I am going to catch a bus down to the free clinic."

"You want me to go with you?" she asked.

"Nah, mom, I got this." He nodded.

She smiled. "Now that's my King."

*****

Miles was embarrassed and bewildered all at the same time. The STD section at the free clinic was jam packed. He must've watched at least thirty high school-aged kids come and go while he waited for over two hours in the large waiting area.

He didn't show it too much when they were together, but he was scared and worried about his mother. He wanted to cry so bad when she told him. He still couldn't believe his own mother was HIV positive. She was so beautiful and healthy looking. And she'd had it for at least 12 years he figured, calculating his youngest brother's age with the timeline she was diagnosed.

"Mr. Malloy, the doctor will see you," the clinic assistant said.

After asking a stream of embarrassing questions, the doctor examined him, before leaving Miles sitting on the examination table.

It was the longest twenty minutes of his life, as Miles prayed and waited for the results of his swab culture.

Finally the doctor walked back in. "Son, you've got Gonorrhea, one of the most common STDs." He extended his arm out to Miles. "Take this paper bag. In it you'll find ten condoms and a bottle of penicillin. Take one pill four times a day for seven days. Do not miss a pill, and do not have sex for at least two weeks."

Gonorrhea? How had one night of pleasure left him with an STD? But when he weighed what could've been the outcome, he couldn't help but breath a sigh of relief.

"You don't have to worry about that," Miles told the doctor. "I won't be doing that again until after I graduate from college. I don't care what people think, or what they say. You will never stick that metal toothpick up me again." He shivered, as he thought of the cotton topped stainless steel toothpick-sized rod that the doctor inserted. "They can talk about me from now until I get married. I am not having sex, period."

Dr. Frazier smiled. "If you only knew how many times I've heard similar statements."

"You've never heard them from me, though, Doc. I'm a straight A student. Ever since first grade I knew what I was going to do. And ever since seventh grade I knew how I was going to do it. And this is the first and last time anyone or anything will stand in my way from being in a position to be the King my mom has always told me I was. She will have that big house with no mortgage, and she will not have to fry anyone's chicken, or take orders from high school and college kids that don't know half of what she does." He nodded. "You best believe, Doc, I am going to be the somebody my momma always tells me I am."

"Sounds like your mother's very special," Dr. Frazier said.

"Special? Doc, my mother is a Queen, and she deserves to be treated like one. My daddy, and none of my siblings' Daddy's took time to recognize it, but I did and I do."

"Do you want Dekalb Medical Center to contact everyone you've been sexually involved with in the last sixty days?"

"Nope, I'll take care of that today, Doc," Miles said before leaving the examination room.

Standing outside of the clinic, Miles decided to call Dreanna one more time before popping up at her house. But this time he called the house number instead of her cell.

"What up?" the woman answered on the second ring.

"Dreanna?"

"Yeah, this she."

"This is Miles. I don't know why you avoided me all day, but that's cool. Anyway, I won't worry you anymore than I have to, but I need to know if you're on the pill. And second, I just left the free clinic, you gave me gonorrhea."

"Little nasty punk. My daughter ain't gave you no disease. If anything, you gave her the VD. And no she ain't on no Birth control pill. She done been on the shot since she was thirteen. Fast tail heffa ain't bringing no more babies up in this house. Hell, I had a hard enough time finding folks to take my other four kids in. On second thought, that tramp might have gave you something, you was the second boy up in her room on prom day. I'm gon' beat her ass for not using condoms. I know I just got her some from the clinic last week. Bye, boy, and don't be callin' my house no more," she said before hanging up the phone.

http://www.cdc.gov/hiv/topics/aa/index.htm
http://www.avert.org/children.htm
http://www.menstuff.org/issues/byissue/teenstds.html

THE MESSAGE

SELF-REFLECTION

1. According to the Center for disease Control, 50 percent of African-American teenage girls are walking around with sexually transmitted infections: Why do you think this is, and what are you going to do about it?

2. Do you come from a single parent household? If your answer is yes, then what are you doing in order to prevent from having a child of your own being raised in a single parent household?

3. When you look at your mother what do you see? When you look at a female at school what do you see? When you look at yourself what do you see?

4. What can you do, what will you do, to prevent from becoming a teenage single parent?

5. Are you comfortable with talking about sex with your parents?

Chapter V

A Mind is a Terrible Thing to Waste

In order to properly educate our children we must have an ideology, which reflects the ideals and aspirations of our people. One component of such an ideology is the importance of seeing the child as a MIND developing in the environment of a physical body in a material world.

-Na'im Akbar

***"Put your hand down, Clown**.*" The nineteen-year-old eleventh grader that sat behind Kwan whispered.

Victor was already mad that he'd been late for class. Now he had to suffer, in the second row behind the new kid, while all his friends sat in the back rows.

Kwan not only ignored him, but instead of just holding his arm straight up in the air, he began waving his hand back and forth.

Ms. Jablonski tried to pretend as if she didn't see Kwan's arm, but at fourteen, Kwan was six feet tall, one hundred eighty pounds, and as he did in all of his classes, he sat in the front row. His was the only black face in the front, although he attended the predominantly black Attucks High School. Having been homeschooled by his father since kindergarten, going to public school required some major adjustments, which Kwan was having trouble with.

THE MESSAGE

Ms. Jablonski looked Kwan's way before pointing. "Mr. Karenga, do you have a question or comment?"

He stood. "Yes, ma'am."

She waved him down. "No need to stand," she said.

"I've been following along with you in the textbook, and if I am correct we are here to be educated, so why all the lies?" he held up the six hundred page blue US History book.

"What would you be referring to, Mr. Karenga?" She didn't try to hide her exasperation.

"Well, for one, you and the text explain how Christopher Columbus discovered America. First, his name was *Christoph,* and second, I don't understand how you can discover a land that is not lost. I mean, when he mistakenly arrived on the shores of this country, people already lived here, so that's like me going to Japan today, and getting a national holiday named after me. I've never been to Japan so I will have discovered it." He spoke with the confidence of someone who knew his history.

The class broke out in laughter.

"Quiet down, class," the teacher reprimanded. A moment later after regaining some semblance of order she continued. "Christopher Columbus was a pioneer and in 1492 he landed on these shores."

"I don't doubt that, but he couldn't have discovered it, because people already lived here.' Kwan shrugged matter-of-factly. "Plus, I don't think it's fair for our parents to pay taxes for public education when we are taught so many lies. I mean there is a national holiday for a man that did not do anything extraordinary, as a matter of fact he accidentally landed in America."

"Okay, thank you for enlightening us, Mr. Karenga. Now class lets go on to chapter 11. Who wants to begin reading?" she asked, not even looking Kwan's way.

He stood up again. “Please excuse me, Ms. Jablonski, but you failed to answer my question, so I will ask another. Why do we celebrate Independence Day, July 4th, when only one party got independence in this country. Blacks were still slaves. So wouldn’t it be more fitting to celebrate Independence Day on September 22?”

Flustered, Ms. Jablonski answered. “I am the teacher. I have a Masters in history and nothing of significance happened in this country on September 22. Now can we please go on with the lesson?”

“I beg to differ, ma’am. September 22, 1862 is when the emancipation proclamation was signed by Abraham Lincoln, although it didn’t go into effect until January 1st, 1863, but it was still the declaration that declared all men and women free, hence independent.”

“I’ll have to look into that, but if you are correct than I don’t know why it’s not recognized as a holiday.” She looked like she just wanted to end the conversation.

“Can you tell me why Abraham Lincoln gets all the credit for freeing the slaves, when he said in a union address that it was his only alternative in order to preserve the union. He, himself, said if there was any other way he wouldn’t free the slaves. The south was making so much money from slave labor that they wanted to separate from the union and form an independent nation.”

“Where are you getting all of this?” she asked.

“Books. I’ve been homeschooled since I was six. My dad refused to send me to public school. He says that if I’m going to know the truth, than I have to be taught the truth, and the best way is to read history from different sources and authors.”

“How do you know what you read is true?” she asked.

"First, I browse through the bibliography to see the sources for the information in the text I am reading. Next I use the Google search engine to cross reference most of what I read, and even then, after reading so many different sources and perspectives, I believe what truths are consistent, and I've only been here a week, but hardly anything in this text is truthful."

"Mr. Karenga, I am the teacher. You are the student, and if you don't like the way I teach and what I teach, you can go to the principal's office and ask to be placed in another class." She pointed to the door.

He got up and proceeded to the door. Whispers of 'Loser,' 'Know it all,' and 'Clown' assaulted his ears as he made it to the door. He looked back at the class and shook his head at all the dark faces that sat in the back row.

Funny how in every class the black kids scrambled to get a seat as close as possible to the back of the class, when we fought so long to sit in the front. The front of theatres, buses, restaurants, everywhere. It was like a modern day invisible Jim Crow era that we are living in, Kwan thought as he made his way to the principal's office.

"Mr. Karenga, you are becoming a regular with us," Miss James, the school administration assistant said as Kwan sat down in the assistant principal's waiting area. She pressed a button on the phone. "Mr. Miller, Mr. Karenga has been sent down again."

"Send him in," the assistant principal said.

Elder Miller was a short man of indeterminable age. He could have been forty or sixty, it was hard to tell by looking at him. He reminded Kwan of a black Sherlock Holmes, wearing a tweed suit every day and walking around with his hands always behind his back. He always seemed to be in deep thought, even when talking to someone.

"Mr. Karenga," Mr. Miller said while pacing his large office. "Kwan Karenga," he repeated while Kwan stood and watched the assistant principal's methodical, slow hands-behind-the back-pacing.

"Have a seat son," he said, extending a hand toward one of the shiny black padded leather chairs in front of his desk.

"Why, may I ask am I given the dubious honor of having you in my presence for the third time in five days?" he asked, still pacing behind Kwan.

"I was questioning the lies that are being taught in our U.S. history books, and are being co-oberated by Mrs. Jablonski."

"That's not what I was told," Mr. Miller momentarily stopped pacing and pointed at his desktop computer. "Ms. Jablonski I'med me. She says you were being disruptive, and you called her a liar."

"In so many words I did call her a liar, but disruptive, I was not, Sir. I merely asked questions as to the validity of what she was reading and teaching."

"The same reason you've been sent to my office the other three times." He put a hand on the young man's shoulder. "Son, you're very intelligent. In over forty years of being in academia, I have never seen anyone like yourself, that's the reason I haven't suspended or expelled you. You are fourteen in the eleventh grade. I am sure that when the scores come back from the CAT, yours will be one of the nation's highest." Mr. Miller walked around and sat on the edge of the dark wood desk and looked Kwan in the eye. "I've been on this Earth for sixty-five years. And I don't agree with a lot of things. I know that our school system is far from perfect, and I know there are some untruths that are being taught, but this is the way of this nation, son. You can not be a rebel in a land full of patriots. It just won't work. You know your history. Look at what happened to every black man that rebelled against the system. Jesus of Nazareth, Hannibal of Carthage, Marcus Garvey, Malcolm X., Dr. Martin Luther King Jr, Asa Phillip Randolph, Paul Robeson, James Baldwin, Medgar Evers, and I could go on. All of them died before their time, all of them forgotten by the people they died for."

"Jesus is not forgotten?" Kwan said.

"Yes he has been. Look at the way Jesus is depicted in our society. A white man with long brown hair. A non-violent, peaceful person. Jesus was a black revolutionary that did not bow down to the system for which he died fighting against. Now, today we have accepted the mystery Jesus that has been put before us. We even celebrate December 25th as his birthday, which is impossible for that to have been his day of birth. For hundreds of years we have been horse whipped into believing a certain way, a way that is not the truth. We've accepted it, this is just the way it is and the way it's always going to be." He stood up and began his methodical pacing behind Kwan again. "You know the truth, Mr. Karenga. Good. Keep it to yourself while you are in public. It is the system that has provided you with books, teachers and a classroom. You have to bite your tongue and just do as you are told while in school. What you do before and after school is your business," Mr. Miller said, before walking back in front of Kwan. "A young man gifted with your height should be participating in sports. I know you play basketball, right?"

"No, sir." Kwan shook his head. "I play education."

"So serious for a young man of your age. Well, in any case, I hope we understand each other, because if we don't, there is always private school, Mr. Karenga." Mr.

Miller opened the door. "Have a good day, Mr. Karenga. I hope we understand each other."

*****

It was Friday afternoon, the school bell had just rung and the mad rush was on. If you didn't move fast enough you where liable to get crushed under the feet of high school kids rushing to get to their lockers and out of the building.

Kwan took his time walking out of the building and to where his bus was due to arrive. He wasn't shocked at what Mr. Miller had told him earlier. His father and the many fathers and mentors that he had studied since he began reading at the age of three had prepared him for the mindset of folks like Mr. Miller, which was the vast majority of black people, he surmised.

"Hey, Punk. I know you hear me, ol' lame-hand-in-the-air-buster."

Kwan removed the backpack from around his shoulders as the name caller approached.

"Sissy boy. You think you so smart."

Kwan opened his bag and took out the book *Last Man Standing: the Geronimo Pratt story*. It was his favorite. A small crowd had gathered around him and Victor, the name caller.

"Hey, Punk, what you gon' do if I bust you upside your head and take that book?"

"You don't have to take it. Here," Kwan extended his arm, "I'll give you the book."

"Punk, I don't want no book." Victor shrugged. "What I'ma do with a dang-on book?"

"I'd appreciate if you would address me by my name, Victor."

"And what you gon' do if I don't?" Victor said.

"Oooooooooohhhhhhhh," the crowd intoned.

Kwan shook his head. "So, let me get this right. You wanna fight me because I stood up for you and everyone in class."

"You ain't stood up for me, fool. You ain't do nothin' but run your mouth."

"Soooooooooo, you're okay with Mrs. Jablonski teaching you lies? You're okay with learning backward?"

"Huh?" Victor frowned up.

"Learning backward. That's what I call it. You have no control over the truth if you don't read. The school books teach that Thomas Edison discovered the light bulb, but they don't tell you that a man who shared your same skin complexion caused that light bulb to light up, Granville T. Woods. And you, Jules."

"Who me?" Victor's sidekick said.

"You're Hispanic, right?" Kwan asked.

"Yeah, so what?"

"The other day in class Mrs. Jablonski was going over how the West was won, and how the U.S. armed forces fought several battles pushing the Hispanics back into Mexico, but what she, nor the U.S. history books spoke of, was how all of those battles were fought on Mexican territory. The California gold rush in the 1800's, Hispanic land, Hispanic Gold, Nevada, Arizona, Texas, where the famed Alamo was taken - all of that is Mexican territory, that was stolen from your people." Kwan pointed to the young Hispanic brother. "Your people were slaughtered, women raped and ravaged in order to steal your history, your land, and now the same descendants that stole your land, have borders and armed patrols preventing you from coming over to land that is rightfully yours. When they do let you come over to the states, they give you green cards. Greencards. Why? Because they know you are green, naïve and won't lift a thought from your head to fight for what is yours. The same as all of us." He waved his left arm in a semi-circle. "This is supposed to be the United States of America, not the United States of White America, Black America, or Hispanic America. Together, Hispanics and African-Americans make up over 25 percent of the population. We helped build this country, with our blood, sweat, tears, and fears. But when it comes to education, our history is so watered down and diluted you would think we have no story in this country, except for that as slaves. And slaves are what we still are because we let others give us our past, present and future. The TV and others shape us. We blindly follow, that's why it's so easy to control us."

"How you mean, dog?" another brother from in the crowd asked.

"Example, this Iraq war. The TV tells us we're fighting against terrorists. Are you a terrorist for protecting your home? You mother? Your children? Has anyone ever seen an insurgent uniform? Another man invades your home and says you can't have guns, and you can't worship a certain way. Now you weren't bothering him. You fight back. Now, who's the terrorist?"

"Ain't never thought of it like that," a young lady from the crowd said.

"That's because we're only given the information the Powers-that-be want us to have." Switching gears Kwan continued, "Right now, they say we're in a recession, right?"

Heads nodded.

"There are no jobs?"

More nods.

"But did you know the oil companies are making record profits? Every day gas prices change. But most of the oil is supposedly controlled by the Middle East. We know it's in the Middle East. Where is Iraq? Where is Kuwait, Pakistan, Afghanistan?"

"The Middle East," Victor answered.

"So, if we are at war with the people who control the oil, than how in a time of a recession can the American oil companies be making record profits in the billions per quarter?" Kwan knew he was getting a little deep for his classmates. But he had a captive audience for once and so he wanted to take advantage of it. "We have to wake up, go out and surf the web for knowledge," he continued. "We have to go to the library read our history, and what's going on around us, because what we read, what we know and learn affects all of us, how we think, how we act, and what we do."

"Okay, okay, break it up," Mr. Miller and two security guards barreled through the crowd of high school kids. "I shoulda' known," Mr. Miller said, shaking his head. "Come with me, Mr. Karenga. I warned you. Now you're fighting and causing a disturbance on school grounds."

Kwan didn't move.

"Mr. Karenga, I said come with me. And all of you disperse. Now! Or I'll have all of you arrested with Mr. Karenga here."

"He wasn't fighting, Mr. Miller," Victor said.

"Mr. Johnson, if I were you I'd be quiet. You stay in enough trouble. I'll say it one last time. Break it up, and go on home, all of you." He waved at the crowd. "It's not the school's fault you opted to miss the school bus, and chose to stay here listening to him," Mr. Miller pointed to Kwan.

"If he's arrested, he'll be kicked out of school," Jules said.

"He should have thought of that before starting this mess," a security guard said.

Victor looked back at the twenty or so kids that had stayed to listen to the fourteen year old. He shrugged, walked up next to Kwan and held his wrists out. "If he goes, I go," Victor said.

"If that's the way you want it, Mr. Johnson," Mr. Miller said sternly.

It started one at a time, then two, three, four at a time until twenty-three kids, white, black and Hispanic, surrounded Kwan, each holding their wrists out. All of them were ready and more than willing to be arrested and expelled if Kwan was arrested and expelled.

Mr. Miller shook his head. He was dumbfounded. As much as he was upset that his day had been disrupted, a part of him felt proud. This was the first time, after all, that he'd seen these young people stand up for what had once been his motto: "If you don't stand for something, you'll fall for anything." And quiet as it's kept, he couldn't be more proud.

THE MESSAGE

SELF-REFLECTION

1. Have you ever asked yourself, why we honor holidays that have nothing to do with us as a people, but we don't honor Dr. Carter G. Woodson's birthday, Booker T. Washington's birthday, Malcolm X's birthday, Granville T. Woods birthday, Marcus Garvey's birthday, Frederick Douglas's Birthday, Richard Allens birthday, Harriet Tubman's Birthday, or any of the heroes and sheroes that helped make it possible for our being here today?

2. For so long we weren't allowed to sit up front on busses, in auditoriums, movie theatres, and other public places. Almost 50 years after the Jim Crow age, we still sit at the back of busses, and worse, at the back of school classrooms where we can't hear and see the teacher as clear as those who sit up front? Why do you think this is?

3. If we helped build this country; if we were responsible for much of it's story, then why do you think Black History isn't equally inclusive in U.S. History, and why do you think we are told lies in school about history, such as the Christopher Columbus lie?

4. Why is knowing your history so important?

5. Why were the slaves freed? And why weren't we told that Abraham Lincoln never wanted the slaves to be freed?

Chapter VI

Slave Mentality

One doesn't wait for the right conditions for revolution. The forces of revolution itself will make the conditions right.

-Che Guewa

"Call me Willie," the medium built man said as he shook hands with Governor William Cabal.

"How 'bout that. You're Willie and I'm William. Have a seat." The Governor of Virginia extended an arm toward an antique high back chair in the parlor of the governor's mansion. "I am so glad you could make it. We've heard that you've been able to do wonderful things with the niggas in the islands," the governor said.

"I have." Willie nodded.

"You must be exhausted from your long journey," the governor said.

"Not at all. My niggas took good care of me. I rested the entire trip," Willie said.

"I knew you were something special when I saw how the slaves treat you. You weren't afraid of them turning on you and throwing you overboard? One man against eight savages." The governor looked at the plain looking man that sat on his left. "I don't see a whip or a gun. Amazing. You mind giving me a little incite into how you control your niggas so well?"

"Sure." He leaned forward. "Well first…"

"Hold on, one second. Clarence," the governor called out.

"Yessuh, Mr. William, suh," the hulking, bright-skinned man answered as he rushed into the parlor. "Clarence, this is Mr. Willie."

"How do, Mr. Willie, suh?" Clarence said, avoiding eye contact with the strange dark, white man that sat next to his master.

"He gon' give us some insight into us better controlling the slaves. Go get a quill, a bottle of ink and a scroll."

Clarence nodded.

"And go get that yella gal we just brought into the house. I need my feet rubbed, while you transcribe what Willie here bestows upon us."

"Yes, suh, Massa, yes suh." The six-foot-four man had a striking resemblance to the governor, as did a couple other slaves that lived at the mansion.

Moments later, Clarence was in the kitchen barking orders. "High yella Wench, I can't b'lieve this here all the work you done did in the last hour. I's the one that got you out them fields, and look at you. Lookin' like a wet dog on yo' hand and knees."

"But Clarence, you's told me to scrub the kitchen flo'. I been at it since you tol' me."

Clarence took two long strides and slapped the young girl so hard she couldn't see straight for a good two minutes. "Get yo' tail up, wash yo' funky behind, get that foot tub, fill it up with tongue-warm water and bring it into the parlor. Massa be good to me. He be good to all us on this here plantation, and I'll kill any nigga myself, fo' I let any y'all take advantage of his graciousness. Now git to gittin' girl, fo' I git massa's whip."

Fifteen minutes later, Clarence was back in the parlor, the young new house slave in tow.

"Willie, I don't know what I'd do without Clarence here. He the best nigga I got. Dang near lost him last year when two unruly niggas got the drop on me. They had me down in the dirt with a noose around my neck. I thought for sure I was gon' meet my Maker any minute when Clarence come outta nowhere, pulled the two off me, and beat them niggas to death with his bare hands. One of them boys musta poked seven holes in Clarence with that darn ice pick, before it broke off in Clarence's rib cage. Later the next week, I was two seconds from shootin' the ol' boy, puttin' him out his misery, when God tol' me to give it one mo' day. Lo and behold the next mo'nin' his fever had broken and here we are today," the governor said.

"Boy, come here and test my water," the governor ordered after he'd already stuck his feet in the gray metal tub.

Clarence got on his knees and stuck his head down in the water, slurped, swigged it around in his mouth before swallowing.

"My feet get numb after a lot of walking, and hot water and a massage wakes them up. But Clarence here tastes the water after I put my feet inside, to see if it's too hot." The governor winked at Willie.

"Just right, Massa, suh," Clarence said, his face still at the governor's feet.

"Go on and sit down ova' yonder." The governor made reference to a wooden chair behind a small desk in the parlor. "You, girl. Gently rub my feet while they in the water," he said to the fifteen-year-old girl that was on her knees in front of the governor.

"Boy, you been whippin' up on my niggas again?" the governor said as he noticed the fresh bruise on the young girl's face.

"I's sorry, Massa, but yous knows how I gets when I feels like a nigga is takin' advantage of you." Clarence diverted his eyes to the floor.

"I know, boy, but this here girl is fresh meat. She ain't been touched. I can't go and give her to Mr. Willie here for the night with that awful bruisin' on her face. After we finish here, you just gon' have to go and get your wife for Mr. Willie."

"Yes, suh." Clarence nodded his compliance.

"Willie, you gon' like that gal my boy married to. She's a little feisty one in the sack, and almost as pretty as a white woman," the governor said, a wicked smile across his face.

"I'm obliged. Now let's get started so we can finish," Willie said. "Lookin' forward to that ol' gal you speakin' of."

"Boy, you ready?" the governor asked Clarence.

"Yes, suh," he said with the smile of good livin' plastered over his face, ink-dipped quill in hand.

"First, you have to understand what a slave is. A slave is one who completely and unconditionally submits their will to another." Willie stood up and began pacing the room with his hands clasped together behind his back. "How do you get one to do this?" Willie asked. "You control the mind of the slave. You make them believe that you are the manifestation of God. You give them their religion. You teach them that whatever they do in this life will have everything to do with them being received in heaven, or hell. You create a visual for them. Niggas love visualization. You show them what heaven looks like, make it the most wonderful place imaginable. And you show them hell." He paused. "Fear. Fear is how you will first begin to get them in order. Not fear of you, but fear of what they can't see. God. The God you create for them."

"I don't know about that. We good Christians down here in Virginia."

"Nothing wrong with that. I dibble and dabble with the Word myself. But the highest law in the land is the Pope's law. His decree. And remember it was the Catholic Church and the Pope who ordained slavery after King Ferdinand and Queen Isabella of Spain asked for his blessing. Niggas are soulless animals. Ain't no hell or heaven for a dog, horse, mule, or a nigga. If anything, you doing God's work by keeping them in line and obedient."

"Makes good sense." The governor nodded his head in agreement.

"Next, you have to use entertainment, games, sex, and whatnot to reward them for a good crop, or some other accomplishment. Give them a prize for their good deeds. But never, by all means, and I mean never," he emphasized, "give them truth. Always entertainment instead of education. Take for instance, that boy." He pointed to Clarence. "You got him writing, and if he can write, he can read. The first way to start a mutiny. The first way to lose control is to teach them to read. You must make them believe with all their heart and soul that reading and writing is useless. Make them believe in you. Make them think that you'll tell them everything they need to know. You give them their understanding. And next is division."

The Governor interrupted. "You keepin' up, boy?"

"Yes suh, Massah suh," Clarence said as he continued writing every word as fast as Willie could get them out of his mouth.

"Where was I?" Willie stopped his pacing and looked around. Seconds passed. No one answered.

"I believes yous said division, suh?" Clarence announced.

"Smart nigga there," Willie said.

"Well, thank you." The governor beamed.

Willie waved a finger in the air. "That is not a compliment. If he wasn't so loyal, I'd suggest you put him down. Remember, a smart nigga should be a dead nigga."

The governor nodded.

"Okay, now back to division. You have to use the One Better system. Pit the light against the dark. Make one better than the other. Pit short against tall, old against young, etc." Again he stuck a finger in the air. "Always, always use them to do the dirty work. No more white overseers. Make them the overseer. Have them beat and whip the others. After the beatings it is you who must show compassion. It is you who must stop the beatings. Make them worship you without them knowing that they are worshipping you. You do this and I guarantee, after a generation or two, maybe three. You won't have to call them nigga, or feed them pigs, and other vile foods, they will call each otha niggas, they will make the pig their favorite dish. They will love you more than they love themselves. They will try and emulate you, your walk, your talk, and they will even kill for you. They will fight on the front lines of wars, and be the first to die for you. Why, because you will be their God."

"What about schoolin'? Ever since Clarence taught hisself how ta read, I noticed an interest in some others wanting to read," the governor said.

Willie waved a hand at the governor. "Remember what I told you. Entertainment. That is your key to thwart any desires of education. Make education, reading, writing, and book learning harder and worse than shoveling snow in bare feet and hands in the coldest of winter. Like I said, do this for a generation or two and it will be in their genes. They will repeat the slave training for hundreds, thousands of years to come. From then on, they will be slaves before they come out of they mammies' wombs. A slave is 100 percent mental, zero percent physical. Control the head, the body will follow. Only thing you must do is continue to be innovative in keeping the slave dependant on you for their beliefs, and understanding."

"What you think about all this boy?" the governor asked his most trusted and intelligent slave.

Clarence looked up, put a hand on his chin and said, "I agrees, suh. We have to divide the niggas. And we's have to use words. Call them names, bad names, and teach them what the names mean, and beat them into using those names, and eventually they will be calling each other those names amongst themselves, using words like nigga like it's a sign of love or somethin'. Heck, suh, they'll even fight if someone tells them to quit using words like nigga. I can see them trying to justify using negative words, when some ol' boys try to come and educate them. Yes, suh." Clarence nodded. "And best, suh, you take a fox hound at birth, treat it like a cat, call it a cat, and by golly he'll begin thinking like a cat. That's what we do with the nigga. Call him a dog. Treat him like a dog, and he will eventually act like a dog," Clarence proudly said.

The governor and Willie nodded their heads in agreement.

Clarence continued. “And the nigga overseer is a genius idea. Fo’ long we might have niggas in law and politics, at least up north that is. That be a good way to find out what niggas is really thinkin’. And that be a good way to control without controlling. The niggas will control each other and report back…”

“You are getting ahead of yourself, Clarence.”

“Yes, suh. Sorry, suh,” Clarence said before lowering his head, like a scolded puppy dog.

*****

The next day, a large group of men were gathered near the James River as Willie took the makeshift stage. It was a beautiful sunny day. The air was clear and smelled clean, when Willie Lynch began his famous oration.

“Gentlemen, I greet you here on the bank of the James River in the year of our Lord, one thousand seven hundred and twelve. First, I shall thank you, the gentlemen of the colony of Virginia, for bringing me here. I am here to help you solve some of your problems with the slaves. Your invitation reached me in my modest plantation in the West Indies where I have experimented with some of the newest and still the oldest method for the control of slaves.” He looked out at the huge crowd of onlookers.

“Ancient Rome would envy us if my program is implemented. As our boat sailed south on the James River, named for our illustrious KING JAMES, whose BIBLE we CHERISH, I saw enough to know that our problem is not unique. While Rome used cords or wood as crosses for standing human bodies along the old highways in great numbers, you are here using the tree and the rope on occasion."

"I caught the whiff of a dead slave hanging from a tree a couple of miles back. You are losing valuable stock by hangings. You are having uprisings, slaves are running away, your crops are sometimes left in the fields too long for maximum profit, you suffer occasional fires, your animals are killed. Gentleman, you know what your problems are; I do not need to elaborate. I am not here to enumerate your problems. I am here to introduce you to a method of solving them."

"In my bag, I have a foolproof method for controlling your slaves. I guarantee every one of you that if implemented, it will control the slaves for at least three hundred years. My method is simple, any member of your family or any OVERSEER can use it." He paused for dramatic effect.

"I have outlined a number of differences among the slaves, and I take these differences and make them bigger. I use **FEAR**, **DISTRUST**, and **ENVY** for control purposes. These methods have worked on my modest plantation in the West Indies, and it will work throughout the SOUTH. Take this simple little list of differences and think about them. On the top of my list is **AGE** but it is only there because it starts with an "A". The second is **COLOR** or shade; there is **INTELLIGENCE**, **SIZE**, **SEX**, **SIZE OF PLANTATION**, **ATTITUDE** of owner, whether the slaves live in the valley, on a hill, east or west, north, south, have fine or coarse hair, or if they're tall or short. Now that you have a list of differences, I shall give you an outline of action- but before that, I shall assure you that DISTRUST IS STRONGER THAN TRUST, AND ENVY IS STRONGER THAN ADULATION, RESPECT OR ADMIRATION."

THE MESSAGE

He pounded the podium as he continued. "The black slave, after receiving this indoctrination, shall carry on and will become self-refueling and self-generating for hundreds of years, maybe thousands. Don't forget you must pitch the old black versus the young black males, and the young black male against the old black male. You must use the dark skinned slaves against the light skin slaves. You must use the female against the male, and the male against the female. You must always have your servants and OVERSEERS distrust all blacks, but it is necessary that your slaves trust and depend on us.

"Gentlemen, these kits are your keys to control, use them. Never miss an opportunity. My plan is guaranteed, and the good thing about this plan is that if used intensely for one year the slave will remain perpetually distrustful."

Authors Note: It is said that William Lynch actually wrote the above the speech in 1772 in a letter to the slave owners.But, there is no evidence that William Lynch ever existed, although there is no question that the Willie Lynch mentality did and does still exists. This letter is one of the major problems of the African-American race today. And with this knowledge we as a race can and will overcome. So with this letter still in your mind I ask that you enlighten someone else and send this letter to as many brothers and sisters. We as a race must start somewhere in learning our problems. What better place than the document that started the destruction of the black race?

REFERENCES

The Willie Lynch Letter and the Making of a Slave by Kashif Malik Hassan-El

Breaking the Curse of Willie Lynch: The science of slave Psychology by Alvin Morrow
http://thetalkingdrum.com/wil.html

THE MESSAGE

SELF-REFLECTION

1. If you had to reduce a people into being slaves, how would you begin the process?

2. If you wanted to begin freeing the minds of a slave, how would you begin this process?

3. Traditions: Look at five traditions/holidays that you celebrate and get on the Internet, or go to your local library and research their origins.

4. Compare institutional slavery to chattel slavery and explain which is worst.

5. The **Preamble to the United States Constitution** is a brief introductory statement of the fundamental purposes and guiding principles which the Constitution is meant to serve. It expresses in general terms the intentions of its authors, is sometimes referred to by courts as reliable evidence of what the Founding Fathers thought the Constitution meant and what they hoped it would achieve.

   We the People of the United States, in Order to form a more perfect Union, establish Justice, insure domestic Tranquility, provide for the common defence, [1] *promote the general Welfare, and secure the* ***Blessings of Liberty to*** **ourselves** ***and our*** **Posterity**, *do ordain and establish this Constitution for the United States of America.* Did the founding fathers mean for the constitution to be equal to all peoples or just them and their children, children's children and so on?

Chapter VII

I Brought You In This World, I'll Take You Out

We wear the mask that grins and lies
it hides our cheeks and shades our eyes
this debt we pay to human guile
with torn and bleeding hearts we smile

Paul Laurence Dunbar

"Let me out right here," Karl said, tapping on Ray-Ray's shoulder.

"Nah," Ray-Ray responded, still slowly driving the Volvo station wagon down the dark street. "I'm droppin' you off where I picked your butt up."

"Man, you play too much. You know how my momma is," Karl said, leaning over the seat.

"I know." He smiled. "That's why I'm droppin' yo' butt off in the driveway. Last time, Ms. Karen kicked yo' ass, in front of all us, remember that CJ?" Ray-Ray said, reaching over to the passenger side and playfully hitting CJ in the chest.

"Fool, you make me drop this blunt, it's gon' be on," CJ said, passing the blunt to Karl. "You wanna hit this one last time before Ms. Karen throw them B's on you?" he joked.

THE MESSAGE

Karl was scared to death, although he'd never let his boys know. It was two-thirty in the morning, way past his midnight curfew, and he was high. Everybody in the world knew his momma wasn't playing with a full fifty-two. Last time he came in past curfew, she ran out in the driveway and dragged Karl out Ray-Ray's momma's car and tore him up. Making it even worse, she had her hands wrapped like a boxer. The next day at school - thanks to his boy's big mouths - he was the story of the day. He was taken out of class and sent to the high school guidance counselor's office, because of the bruise his momma left over his right eye. It was actually his fault that she beat him so bad. He didn't know what he was thinking, hitting his momma back.

Mrs. Brand from Child and Family Services was waiting when he had gotten to the counselor's office. She'd asked about the bruise and the rumors of child abuse, which he staunchly denied.

"Nah, Man, keep goin'. Swear on my life, if you pull into my driveway, I'm gon' choke the hell outta you," Karl said from the back seat as they slowly passed his house.

"Ah, man, yo' momma sleep. Ain't a light on in the house," CJ said. "Dude, I don't know why yo' momma be trippin' so hard. I mean, you fifteen. In three years you'll be grown. Look at me and Ray-Ray. Ms. Jean, Ray-Ray momma let him push the whip, and he just got his license. Neither of our mommas be trippin'."

"Yeah, they know the deal. We men, and they treat us like men," Ray-Ray said. "We ain't got no curfew. I don't know what a curfew is."

"Y'all right. I'ma' man. Momma don't understand the way of the world. Stuff done changed since she was growin' up. She a woman. She don't know what it is to be a man."

Ray-Ray stopped the car two houses past Karl's. "So, you want me to drop you off right here or you gon' man up and let me turn around and pull into the driveway?"

Karl didn't say anything. He just opened the door.

"That's what I thought ol' scary-behind, hen-pecked momma's boy," CJ teased as Karl gently closed the back door, and began the long, heart pounding, one minute journey, jogging past two neighbors' houses and into his driveway.

Once at the side door, he took out a small vial of *Obsession For Men* oil that he bought from a Muslim kid at school. He turned the vial up and began bathing his hands and face. He smelled his shirt and hands. Now, satisfied that he no longer smelled like weed, he walked into the backyard, lifted an old spare tire and took out the Listerine he'd hidden. After rinsing out his mouth he straightened his clothes, walked back to the carport door and slowly inserted the key.

Out of the six or seven times he stayed out past curfew, he'd only been caught once, and that was enough, but why did he still do it?" he asked himself. *Dumb question*, he thought. CJ and Ray-Ray. They were his boys and they always kicked it at Golden Glide on Saturday night. Always the life of the party, they were known as the three Amigos. And the girls. They were plentiful and they loved the way the three put on a skating show at Golden Glide. Nobody could even come close to putting it down like they did. And sing… man, Ray-Ray could blow. They'd won every talent show they'd ever entered.

Suddenly the kitchen light came on, blinding Karl.

A broken broom stick was at his chin. "Boy, you think I'm something to play with?" his mother said.

"Nah, ma, I was-"

"You was just nothin'. Boy, I was worried sick." She paused. Sniffed the air. Leaned in, sniffed him. Stepped back. Looked at his half sleep red eyes. "Karl Jamal Johnson. You been smokin'?"

"Huh?"

"Huh, hell. You heard me." She pushed the broomstick further under his chin.

"Mom?"

"Don't mom me." She shook her head in disappointment. "I can't believe you."

"Nah, mom." He shook his head. "I wasn't smokin'."

She pushed the broken broom handle even further up his chin.

"Mom?"

"You think I'm stupid. How many times I told you that you ain't doing nothin' I haven't done or seen. You smell like a perfume factory, and your eyes are red as a fire truck."

"I was around some folks that were smoking, uhm, in the, uh, uh, parking lot at Golden Glide, at the skating rink."

She slapped him so hard everything went red. "Try me again. Lie to me one more time."

He tensed up and bit his lip.

"Unball your fists." She said looking at his fists that were twice the size of hers.

Karen Johnson was five-five, one-hundred forty-pounds. Karl towered over his mother at five-eleven. He was slim with an athletic build.

"Mom, I'm fifteen, not ten. Why you always-?"

"You raisin' your voice at me?"

He didn't say anything. Just breathed loudly.

"Boy, I brought you in this world and as God is my witness I'll take you out this world." She shook her head.

"Hell no. The streets ain't gon' take none of mine. If I gotta bury you, I might as well kill you. You on a death mission anyway. Hangin' out in them streets, getting' high, doin' God knows what, with God knows who."

"Momma, it ain't… I mean it isn't like that. We was just skating and kickin' it in the parking lot of Golden Glide with everybody else. All the kids hang out at Golden Glide and go to the Kroger parking lot on Candler Road."

"The same Kroger parking lot where that boy got shot, last month? The same parking lot where kids go, *after* the police clears everyone out of the skating rink parking lot?" she said, still holding the broken broomstick to her eldest son's chin.

"I'm the only fifteen-year-old man with a curfew."

"*Man*!" She paused, looking him up and down. "*Man!* So, you a man now, huh?" she asked with one hand on her hip. "What bills you paying? What kind of example are you making for Kevin? Your little brother idolizes you, a future druggie."

"Mom, you doin' too much. You don't understand how it is. You're a woman. Things are different growing up a young man."

She pulled the broomstick back. "You right. I don't know how it is being a young man, but I know how it is being a single parent. My momma was a single parent. I lost a brother to the streets. Shot at an 'over 21' club, when he was seventeen. And now my other brother, your Uncle Kalvin, is somewhere getting high. He never was the same after Keno got killed." She shook her head. "I will give my life or take your life before I let the streets have you."

"I'm not Uncle Kalvin, Mom."

"Boy, just get outta my face before I do something to you. Go on." She fell to her knees and began crying. "I said go!"

"But, ma?"

"Go!" she shouted between tears.

Karl couldn't sleep. His mother breaking down was worse than any beating or punishment. It tore at his soul to see his mother like that. *She just didn't understand,* he thought before crying himself into an unfitful sleep.

Early the next morning, Karl got up, cooked breakfast for him, his mother and his thirteen-year-old brother.

"Momma, Kevin, wake up!" he shouted. "Breakfast is being served in the Johnson household."

Sunday was a good day. The family had gone to church and it seemed as if the events from last night were forgotten. No punishment. No beat down. Nothing. *Well, except for momma's breakdown,* he thought as he lay in bed waiting for sleep. This week was the big week, and Karl was anxiously awaiting the letter in the mail that would change his and his boys' lives in ways that he couldn't begin to imagine.

On Thursday, after getting off the school bus he had to run to stop the mailman from backing out of the driveway. He made it just in time to sign the receipt, before the mailman handed him the certified letter. His heart was about to pop out of his chest as he stared at the eight-by-eleven white envelope. As bad as he wanted to open it right there, he didn't. CJ and Ray-Ray should be with him as he read it. He decided not to tell anyone until morning.

Friday morning was filled with storms. *April Showers,* Karl thought as he waited at the school bus stop.

He took out the certified letter, and rubbed his fingers over the name it was addressed to. *The Three Gees.*

Thirty minutes later, the three best friends were shooting the breeze and crackin' yo' momma jokes, as they posted up at their normal gathering spot under the awning at the back of the school, the best place to check out all the honies that were getting off the school buses.

"I, being the leader, founder, and most talented member of the Three Gees, hereby," he pulled the envelope out of his London Fog raincoat, "present *the letter*."

"What it say, fool?" CJ snatched at the letter, only grabbing air as Karl pulled it out of CJ's reach.

"Too slow," he said.

"Stop playin'. Open it," Ray-Ray said before pulling out his cell phone. "Don't make me call Ms. Karen and tell her what you were doing and what time you got home Saturday, I mean *Sunday morning*."

Karl patted his chest. "Son, I got this. I'm the man of the house. Momma caught me, and I just had to explain the facts of life to her. Her trippin' days are over."

"So, you like Mandela, huh?" Ray-Ray said.

"Mandela?" Karl and CJ questioned at the same time.

"It took twenty-seven years for him to be freed, and it took fifteen years for your warden momma to let you out," Ray-Ray said, laughing.

"Shut up, Crackbaby," Karl shot back.

"Will you two chill for a minute? Dang. Open up the letter man," CJ said to Karl.

"Okay, Okay," he said, carefully tearing the manila envelope at the edge.

"Yes! Yes! Double yes!" The boys shouted and danced in the rain after hovering next to one another reading the letter.

Karl took out his phone and called his mother.

"Hello?"

"Ma! We did it! We made it! Don't go to work. Quit your job. The Three Gees will be appearing on the 2010 season of 'American Idol.' It's a wrap."

"I knew you'd make it. I'm so proud of you all. Where is Charles and Raymond?"

"They right here."

"Put me on speaker phone, Son."

He did as he was told.

"Boys, I'm so proud of you, and I have no doubt that you will win and be greater than you even imagined."

"Thank you, Ms. Karen," the boys said.

"Now you know we gotta celebrate tonight," CJ said after Karl pressed the End button on his cell. "You think you can get the whip?" CJ asked Ray-Ray.

"Man, nah. Momma takin' it in for servicing today."

"The brakes?" Karl asked.

"Yep," Ray-Ray answered.

"Brakes don't take long. She should be good before the end of the day," CJ said.

"Her appointment at the dealership ain't until six-thirty, after she get off work," Ray-Ray said, as the boys walked inside the building.

"Man, you need to sing in one of your girl's ears. Get them to loan us one of their whips," Karl said.

"Yeah, bust out in some Luther or some Marvin Gaye," CJ said. "These new school broads don't know nothin' 'bout that. They'll melt, you sing some *Distant Lover*, some *House is not a Home* to them."

"Call up one of them college chicks that be sweatin' you. Sing somethin' in they ear. Man, we have to go out," Karl added.

"I gotta better idea. That buster, Wayne, momma's new boyfriend, be tryin' to play daddy, now I'm gon' let him," Ray-Ray said. "He has to bring momma home from the dealership. That's when I'll show them the letter and beg to use his ride."

"I can't wait to kill the audition. Usher, Chris Brown, they all have to move over. We gon' be the next New Edition on skates," Karl said before they gave each other a pound before splitting up and heading to homeroom.

*****

It was still pouring outside at seven o'clock that evening when Karl and CJ clicked Ray-Ray in on the three-way.

"Man, that crab trippin' about the weather. He talkin' 'bout, he can't let me go out in all this rain. The fool got me confused with one of his own kids," Ray-Ray said speaking of his mother's boyfriend.

"Even after you showed them the letter. Don't he know if he play his cards right with your momma, he'll be set for life?" CJ said. "This time next year, we gon' be signed to some big record label. They gon' have to increase the size of concert stages all around the country so we can do what we do on skates and with three microphones."

"Obviously, he don't see the big picture," Ray-Ray said. "That's okay, though. I'll get the Volvo."

"I thought it was in the shop," Karl said.

"Nah, it was raining so bad, momma caught a cab to work, and her hater-crab boyfriend picked her up. She didn't trust the brakes to make it to work and to the dealership in the rain."

THE MESSAGE

"Did you ask her if you could get the whip?" CJ asked.

"Be for real. With that crab boyfriend of hers hatin', I know she'd say no. But that's okay, I already stole her spare key. By, nine o'clock they gon' be up in momma's room glued to the TV, watching some movie. That's when I'm gon' make my move. You crackbabies just be ready, cause it's off and poppin' tonight."

"What we gon' do for money?" Karl asked. "I'm broke."

"You always broke," CJ said.

"Only 'cause yo' momma ain't came by with her check," Karl shot back.

"Nah, yo' momma done smoked up her check," CJ rebutted.

"I always have to come through for you sorry fools. Why do I even deal with either of you?" Ray-Ray asked.

"Because we let yo' good-singin' butt roll with the two coolest cats in Georgia," Karl said.

"I'll take care of the bread. I'll just call up Trina and Renee. They always good for a few dollars," Ray-Ray said, showing his dimples and flashing his Colgate smile.

"Cool, well let me get to workin' on momma now," Karl said, hanging up before his boys could crack on him about asking his mother to let him hang out.

Minutes later, he laid across his mother's bed with her and his little brother. "Momma, when I become famous, the first thing I'm going to do is buy you the baddest MTV Cribs house ever. You deserve that and so much more," Karl said. "Not too many mothers would sacrifice their lives for their kids like you have. I know I been messing up lately, but I'm sorry, and understand that I have to do better and be an example for Kev, and everyone. After all, I'm about to be in the public limelight."

"That's a responsible thing to say. Maybe there is hope for you yet," she said, rubbing the top of Karl's head as he laid across her legs pretending to watch an earlier taping of "Oprah."

He sat up in the bed and looked directly into his mothers eyes. "Momma, I really am going to do right. I'm gonna make you proud."

"Son, I'm already proud, and I thank God every night for blessing me with the two greatest sons in the world."

He hugged his mother. "Mom, I love you so much. I hope I die before you, 'cause I don't wanna live without you," he said.

She pushed him back. "Okay, what do you want?"

"Why do I have to want something in order to spend some quality time and share some love with the number one mother in the world."

"I know you, Karl Jamal Johnson," she said, looking into her son's eyes.

"Well, momma, it's like winning the lottery. Like one in a million. We just got the news that is going to change our lives forever and me, CJ and Karl wanna go out and celebrate."

She nodded her understanding.

"So." He crossed his fingers and held his breath a second. "I can go?"

"No."

"Huh?"

"What part of no don't you understand? The N or the O?"

"But, ma?"

"But ma, nothing." She smiled. "The greatest mother in the world has to continue making the greatest decisions in the world in order to keep my greatest mother title. It's too nasty out and I can't believe Raymond's mother is letting him use her car in all this rain."

"Raymond's *mother* understands the importance of us going out to celebrate. She gave him her spare key and some money for us to have a good time," he lied. "And CJ's mother gave him some money and her blessing to have a good time on such an important evening."

"I'm not Raymond's or Charles's mother. I'm your mother. And the answer is still no."

Karl jumped off the bed and made sure he was out of slapping reach, before shaking his head. "You a trip. You just don't want me to have no fun. I might as well be dead," he said, marching off to his room.

"Boy come back here! Right now!" she said.

A few seconds later he was back inside his mother's bedroom. "What?"

"*What?* Negro, have you lost your mind?" She jumped off the bed. "Who are you speaking to in that tone? And surely I didn't hear you say *what* to me."

Karl just stared at his mother with rage in his eyes.

She held out her hand. "Your cell phone."

He didn't move.

"Your phone, boy! Give it to me!"

"But..."

"Say one more word. Just one." She pointed a finger at him. "And it will be your Playstation, and maybe a tooth or two."

He handed her his phone before stomping off to his room. Minutes later he laid across his bed, seething. He couldn't wait 'til he turned sixteen and had a big record contract. He'd move out, get his own place, and he'd make her beg for him to come back and buy the dream house he'd promised.

*****

Saturday and Sunday had passed. The suspense was killing him. He couldn't wait to hear the happenings of the weekend. He'd been totally cut off from civilization the past couple days. He'd only left his room to use the bathroom and for food. He hadn't had any contact with the outside world the entire weekend. CJ and Ray-Ray probably had the time of their lives Friday night, he thought as he left the house for school that Monday morning.

It was a beautiful sunny, April morning. He decided to walk the two miles instead of catching the school bus. By now everyone knew about "American Idol." And everyone probably wondered why he didn't show up at Golden Glide this weekend to gloat in the glory of the upcoming appearance on national TV.

He lost track of time as he daydreamed and took his time walking. He'd gotten to school right as the homeroom bell rang. His boys weren't at their usual spot. *That's odd,* he thought as he hurried to homeroom before the late bell rang.

Everyone looked at him crazy as he slung his backpack over his shoulders and took a seat, right as the announcements began.

The principal was actually making the announcement, not the usual perky cheerleader who started their day everyday. Her tone was somber. "By now many of you have heard," she began, "and in case you haven't, I am deeply sorry to say that two of our own, Raymond Jerome

Mcafee, and Charles Joplin died after driving a Volvo station wagon into an eighteen wheeler on the I-20 interstate."

The rest of the announcement was a blur. All Karl heard after that, was one of the students behind him saying that Ray-Ray and CJ had been drinking and smoking at some party earlier that evening. He couldn't believe his friends were gone. And even more, he couldn't believe his life had been spared – by a mother's love and determination to save her son from the streets.

SELF-REFLECTION

1. Have you ever smoked or been around others smoking or doing drugs? If so, was the feeling you got worth risking your freedom, your health, and your future.

2. How well do you know the person or persons you smoke with? How well do you know their suppliers, and the suppliers of their suppliers? If the drug dealers are already selling drugs poisoning the user, how do you know they aren't putting in other chemicals in drugs, that could kill you?

3. Name and explain five positives you get out of doing drugs? Okay, name four? Okay, name three? Two? One? If you can't come up with any, than what rational reason would you continue to do drugs or hang around with others who do?

4. I agree. Marijuana is a plant that grows in nature. It's organic, an herb, so why is it illegal and wrong to smoke? A fox glove is a beautiful flower. It puts you in the mind of a rose, mixed with a garden lily. But the foxglove is extremely poisonous. Poison Ivy is a plant. And if you touch, inhale, eat anything that alters you body and mind, would that plant not be poisonous?

5. From this day forward how are you going deal with peer pressure. You out at a club, ballgame, or school dance, your boys are passing the blunt, what you gon' do?

Chapter VIII

City of Bling

When a person places the proper value on freedom, there is nothing under the sun he will not do to acquire that freedom. Whenever you hear a man saying he wants freedom, but in the next breath he is going to tell you what he won't do to get it, or what he doesn't believe in doing in order to get it, he doesn't believe in freedom.

-Malcolm X

Never in history has one person brought so many people to Madison Square Garden. After only five years on the Rap scene, Bo Jack Jones had blown up bigger than Tupac and Biggie together. If Michael Jackson is the King of Pop, then Bo Jack Jones is the King of Rap.

Street vendors sold City of Bling T-shirts, Goon Squad skull caps, and imitation platinum bicycle neck chains and handcuff wrist bracelets, like the ones Bo Jack Jones had made so famous over his short career. The 2010 City of Bling concert was a promoter's dream. It had sold out the first day tickets had gone on sale six months ago back in January. Kids had come from as far as Chicago to see Bo Jack Jones do his thing.

Every major news network from Fox News, to CNN was there to cover the record-setting concert. Record setting, because Bo Jack Jones was the only act performing at the concert. The third album, *The Revolution of the Bling* from the young phenom, Bo Jack Jones had been number one on the billboard charts for a record twenty-four weeks. The songs *A Hundred Grand Draped Around My Neck*, and *The City of Bling* have been swapping places at number one and two respectively, on the charts since their debut release back in November of '09.

Bo Jack's crew, The Goon Squad were in the oversized Madison Square Garden dressing room passing blunts, getting mellow while they awaited their leader. All thirteen members of the Goon Squad were brothas Bo Jack had grown up and did crime with back in his drug dealing, car jacking, and robbing days. And they all came up as he did, in The East Lake Meadows project housing apartments in East Atlanta. Little Vietnam was the name that most people knew the dilapidated and drug infested apartments by, largely in part because of the terror and havoc Bo Jack and his boys had reigned on the small project housing community. But, all had been forgotten after his first album dropped four years ago. Back then, *Ballin' for Life* had made Bo Jack Jones an overnight sensation, with songs like *Saggin' and Baggin*, and *Smoke til ya Choke* skyrocketing to the top of the charts.

By the age of twenty-three, he'd been arrested twenty-five times from everything to assault, attempted murder, drug possession, and armed robbery. Only two charges had ever stuck thanks to his high powered attorneys and his boys taking the fall for him.

Twenty-two years ago, at the age of five after hearing N.W.A's, 1988 hit *Straight Outta Compton*, it was a wrap. That's what inspired him to live, dress and emulate the people and the stories that N.W.A. spoke about in their lyrics. Not only did he embrace the black gangster drug culture, but he tirelessly worked at his rhyming and vocal skills while amassing millions in the illegal drug trade. But now those days were behind him. *Far behind him,* he thought as he waddled into the hallway bathroom looking like a human penguin with his pants hanging down at his knees.

Ahh, what a feelin', he thought as he let loose in the restroom's urinal.

The bathroom door burst open. Two Madison square security guards rushed in, wearing Bo Jack Jones signature black Goon Squad ski masks over their heads. "Fool, you know what it is?" a Madison Square Garden security officer said with a gun pointed at the head of Bo Jack.

"What the…? Bayboy," Bo Jack turned around, zipping up his pants, "you know who I am?"

"Yeah, I know who you is. That's why we here, fool," the security guard said.

The other guard walked up to Bo Jack. "Like your song say, A hundred thousand dollars draped around your neck." He held out his hand. "Give it up, or give it to God." The robber put the nine to Bo Jack's head. "One way or anotha you gon' unass that platinum and ice from around your neck and wrists."

Bo Jack shook his head. He didn't even attempt to remove the platinum bicycle chain with the diamond studded cross with his image engraved in the middle. He looked down at the platinum and diamond studded handcuffs he sported around his wrists. Right as he looked back up at the two guards, a loud noise exploded in his ears, followed by a bright light that blinded him, causing the young phenom to fall back into the urinal, he'd just used.

****

"Ahhhhhhhhhhhhh," Bo Jack screamed, as he arched his back.

"Boy, git yo black ass up out that dirt, and get back to pannin' 'fore I give you ten more lashes," the tall white man said, shaking his head, as he pointed the whip at Bo Jack. "You good for nothin' lazy savages are all the same," the man dressed in old school throwback military regalia said as he walked away.

Bo Jack stood up and looked around with a look of confusion shrouding his face. "The bathroom. The concert. My bling," he said feeling for his necklace and looking at his bare wrists.

A young boy grabbed Bo Jack's arm, "Hurry, pan, pan," the boy, who was no older than seven or eight, said in some foreign dialect that he amazingly understood.

"Where? What? How?" Bo Jack shook his head. "Where am I?" he asked speaking in the same foreign language that the boy spoke in.

"Work, work," the boy said bending over, filling a cake-dish like tin pan with dirt and shaking it around letting the sandy dirt granules fall through to the ground. "Work, work, Colonel Jones will," he made a chopping motion, "cut your dingles off if he see you not panning."

"Dingles?"

"Yes." The boy pointed to Bo Jacks testicles.

Bo Jack looked down, for the first time noticing he was naked, he attempted to cover up with his hands. "Where are my clothes? Where are your clothes?"

"Clothes?" The boy laughed. "We are not allowed to wear clothes in the mines."

Bo Jack looked up and around. There were hundreds, maybe thousands of naked black folks. Women, men, and children panning for as far as his eyes could see in the desert sun. "There must be some mistake," Bo Jack said dropping his pan on the dirt and walking toward the white horse that the man that lashed him sat on.

"No, No, come back, don't go," the young boy's pleas fell on deaf ears as Bo Jack continued walking.

"Sir?" The Colonel turned his horse around and looked down on the naked six-foot tall young man in front of him. "I don't know who you are, how I got here, and what type operations you runnin' but, I'm Bo Jack Jones, and I…"

Before he could get another word out, the Colonel slung his twelve foot whip from his hip, the leather wrapping itself around Bo Jack's neck. "Now you ridicule me," he pointed to himself, "Colonel Beauregard Jackson Jones III, now you will dig your own grave at sunrise." The whip was secured around Bo Jack's neck as the horse began to slowly gallop through the sand and dirt fields that burned Bo Jack's bare feet. Bo Jack had seen the movie "Roots," and others that depicted stories of slavery and human bondage, but nothing came close to what he was seeing now. At least eighty percent of the workers were children. Several times while walking through the fields behind Colonel Jones's horse, he'd witnessed little girls no older than his twelve-year-old sister, being beat with leather whips, and the stench of urine, feces and death permeated the air everywhere he stepped.

Dead bodies. He saw pits with children's dead bodies stacked on top of each other with a thick white powder on top and around them. *What kind of people would do this to children*, he wondered?

It seemed like he'd walked forever, when the horse came to an abrupt halt a couple hour later. Bo Jack was about to faint. He was dehydrated from throwing up in the intense heat. An endless stream of tears trailed behind him for the seven miles he'd walked. The tears weren't for the pain he felt around his neck or in his bleeding and sore feet, but the pain he felt in his heart and soul, for the living and dead bodies that filled the vast dirt plantation.

Bo Jack felt as if he were floating in a haze of hell. "That's it. I'm in hell," he deliriously mouthed as the large white man dismounted and removed the whip from around Bo Jack's neck.

"Put him with the others," he heard the Colonel say.

"What was his crime, my Lord," a man with a cross around his neck asked.

"Blasphemy," the Colonel said. "He introduced himself as me, shortening my namesake to Bo Jack Jones."

"Yet, he still lives?" the man asked.

"Look at him. Large, good digging arms. Why waste him before we can get some work out of the savage?"

"Heathens, all of them. He will dig the death pits until he collapses and then, I shall shoot him myself, for such disrespect," the man in black said.

"Thank you, Father," the Colonel said, addressing the man in black.

Father? Bo Jack, could not believe what he'd just heard.

Moments later, the Colonel was gone. Bo Jack walked with shackles on his feet and hands. "What kind of person are you?"

THE MESSAGE

"I'm a man of Christ," the priest said fingering the gold and diamond studded cross he wore around his neck, as he led Bo Jack to a small dome-like mud dwelling. "In you go," the priest said, as Bo Jack ducked his head and collapsed onto the dirt floor of the mud prison.

He heard the sound of crickets chirping. His eyes slowly fluttered. It was still hot, but not nearly as hot as it was. He turned his head toward the bars on the mud hut. It was dark outside. He was weak, and disoriented, but he felt a hundred times better, as he drank from the tin cup a teenage boy held to his burnt and dry lips.

"Eat," another boy said, pushing something into his mouth. "You must eat, so you can pray, for the souls of the Queen's army."

Hope. *Finally,* he thought as he chewed. After swallowing the tough meat, he asked. "What is this?"

"Rat." We eat whatever we can trap inside the tomb," a boy said referring to the small dark hut they were in.

Bo Jack coughed and tried to get the rat meat to come back up.

"No, don't. The meat will give you strength. It is either eat or starve," the boy that held his head in his lap said.

"So what about this army? Who are they? How soon before they come find us?" he asked.

The boys laughed. "No," the one that held his head in his arms said. "We are not lost. The army is. We pray for their souls. We know Allah. Our blessings will be in the hereafter. It is these men, the army around us, with hearts of stone that we pray for. They speak of God. But they know not what they speak. It is the Shaitan (Satan) that has closed their souls."

"What? Are you serious? Pray for them. The only prayer I'll be praying is for a knife so I can stick it in as many of them as I can."

"Such hatred in your words," the boy said.

"Hate ain't even close to what I feel," Bo Jack said. "I seen what they've done. How can you sit here and be calm? How can you even fix your lips into forming the words, *pray for them devils*? Kids, man. I seen so many kids, beaten, dying, and dead in shallow open graves as I walked here," he cried. "Why? Why?"

"The shiny crystal rocks," another boy said. "They take us from our homes. Murder our families, before bringing us here to work until we die of exhaustion and are reunited with our mothers, fathers, sisters and brothers in the Jenna."

"Jenna?" Bo Jack asked.

"The heavens," another answered.

"How can you pray for them? They stealing your bling, I mean diamonds, killing your family, and working you to death to mine diamonds."

"That is correct?" the boy that held his head a minute ago said.

"But you wanna spend your last moments together praying for them? Man, ya'll on crack."

"What is crack?" the boy asked.

"It's a drug. You know, something you put in your body that makes you escape reality."

"Oh, drink. Yes, they gave our ancestors drink. Lots of drink. It made them dance, shout, and fall to the ground," one boy said.

"They who?" Bo Jack asked.

"The priests and missionaries that came before the army arrived. For the next two generations our people drank and were taught about a great white man that was coming to rescue us. Jesus the Christ. They explained to the elders that my tribe the Zulu were kings of kings, sent by God to rule over the other main tribes of my region. The Twa and the mountain dwelling Bantu people. A hundred years later, while the civil war between the Twa, Bantu and my tribe the Zulu was going on, the white armies showed up and began killing the elders of all the tribes, and forcing us, the young to mine the desert fields of Sierre Leone, make us work until we die of exhaustion."

"How can you not hate them after what they have done, what they are doing?" Bo Jack asked.

"Hate? What is hate? Can it move a stone? Can it heal the sick? No." The boy shook his head. "Hate can do nothing but drive you to feel and do things that are not ordained by Allah. So, instead of hate, we love. We love Allah, with everything we have. We love Him so, that we pray that even the evilest of men find their way to Him before their souls are lost to Shaitan's hellfire."

"Hold on, back up," Bo Jack said. "How long have you lived like this?"

"Two, three hundred years. Maafa," the boy said.

"Maafa?"

"Maafa is holocaust."

"You been dying for hundreds of years over diamonds, little crystal rocks?"

The boy nodded.

"And before you die, the way your ancestors have died, you pray for your killers?"

He nodded. "Prayer is peaceful hope, and protest against the evil in men. It is the only way we know to fight the Shaitan. Allah hears our prayers, and when it is time, He will act on our behalf as long as we don't turn away from

Him. Our reward in the hereafter is so far greater then our suffering in the now. Our prayer is for Allah to rid the evil from the hearts of our white oppressors."

"Do you know what happens to the diamonds you mine?" Bo Jack asked.

"No," the boys said.

"They are set in necklaces, rings, and bracelets and sold as jewelry. The people where I am from pay a lot of money to wear them on their necks, wrists, fingers, toes, and ears."

"What? You mean the crystals are not used to harbor energy, or to heal people?"

Another boy interrupted. "We are being slaughtered by the hundreds of thousands so others can wear our blood as ornaments?"

"Does your tribe know about us? Our suffering." the boy that held his head asked.

Tears dropped onto the dirt floor. "No." Bo Jack shook his head in shame. All the diamonds he'd bought and stolen. Little white rocks. White rocks that symbolized marital commitment. All a lie. Blood diamonds, this was the City of Bling, the true City of Bling. One that his lyrics didn't begin to describe. One that he wished he'd known about, twenty-two years ago when he heard his first N.W.A. record, *Straight Outta Compton*. If Ice Cube, Dr. Dre, Yella, and Eazy-E, were sent back in time like he had been, would they have rapped about Maafa, and the diamond trade? Would *Straight Outta Compton*, be changed into *Straight Outta Sierre Leone*.

If I had one more chance. Just one, he thought as he mentally prepared to pray for the first time in years. The difference in his prayer and the others was, he wasn't praying for the souls of the evil. He got onto his knees, opened his hands and asked God for one more chance.

"Throughout history, it has been the inaction of those who could have acted, the indifference of those who should have known better, the silence of the voice of justice when it mattered most, that has made it possible for evil to triumph."

-Haile Selassie

http://www.diamondsforafricafund.org/realdiamondfacts/home.htm

http://www.africanholocaust.net/html_ah/holocaustspecial.htm

http://ipsnews.net/africa/interna.asp?idnews=16367

SELF-REFLECTION

1. How can buying and wearing expensive rocks, shaped into *nooses*, I mean neck chains, chokers and *handcuffs*, I mean bracelets, and *shackles*, I mean ankle bracelets, and rings make you a better person? And if you can't answer that, then why do we rob, steal, kill, and spend our hard earned money on expensive jewelry?

2. Do you think Black women will still want a diamond wedding ring, or anything made with diamonds, after you explain to them about the history of diamond mining?

3. What will you say to your boys when they wear that fake or real Jacob watch with the diamond bezel or the diamond face on the chain around their neck?

4. How do you feel about diamonds now that you have read and hopefully did your own research into the history of diamonds?

5. Can you name one African-American owned diamond company?

THE MESSAGE

Chapter IX

Chocolate M&M's

Ten thousand fools proclaim themselves
into obscurity, while one wise man
forgets himself into immortality.

-Martin Luther King Jr.

"Forty-five years. Can you believe it's been that long?" the man said to one of his dearest friends.

"Ah, you're still a baby. I've got you by twenty-five years, son."

Both men looked up as the final member of their three-man group came floating in.

"As usual, you're late," the leader and eldest member of the three spoke.

"Musta been dreamin' again," the other member said.

"By any means necessary. A dream is where it all begins," the latecomer retorted.

"Can you shorten your dreams, so you can be on time from now on?" the eldest member asked.

"I'm always on time," the late straggler replied. "It's you two who are early."

"By the looks of things we are all late," the younger of the two men that sat at the table said as he looked down.

"Will you please hurry so we can get started?" the eldest member of the newly formed council said to the youngest member.

"Can a brotha hang up his wings?"

"Come on, Martin get with the times. Just think it into being and your wings will be on the wing rack. You are always doing things the hard way," Marcus, the eldest member said.

"I like being in my old body, and I like manually doing things."

"You been dead forty years and you still haven't made any progress," Malcolm said.

"Forty-two." Martin corrected him while taking a seat. "How can I progress, when the world has regressed so?" Martin said as he looked down at the world through the table they all sat around.

Marcus nodded. "Isn't it a shame?"

"That's why we're here," Malcolm said.

"No." Martin pointed at Malcolm. "You are why we are here. "

"My mother always said be careful what you ask for, you might just get it," Marcus said, looking at Malcolm.

"Don't look at me." He pointed. "Martin started me on this mission. It wasn't until you were reborn in the light of heaven that I began asking Him to let us intercede," Malcolm said.

"I know, and you've been begging Him for over forty years for this chance. You know how He is. He does things on His time, not yours," Marcus said, "How many times have I told your impatient behind?"

Not wanting to hear Marcus go into a State of the Union address, Malcolm conceded, "Okay, you're right. Now let's assess the problems."

"Lets begin by going back and taking a quick peak at the city of Sodom before He destroyed it," Marcus said looking down through the glass table. "See." He pointed. "Right there, you have greed and envy. The two things that motivate most people to act. Who is the author of greed and envy?" Marcus asked. "Satan." He answered his own question. "Look at all the confusion, gentlemen," Marcus said looking down at all the people aimlessly moving in different directions without purpose. "They are lying, whoring, killing, stealing, among other things."

"Fast forward to today June 12, 2010." Martin waved his arm across the table. "Now look at the people of the United States. Same thing."

Malcolm shook his head. "Why didn't they listen? Why are they so blind?"

"Greed and envy," Marcus answered.

"The answers. All of them can be found inside the problem. Simple math. Common sense," Malcolm said.

"Common sense is not common as you can see," Martin said.

"The few that do fight for justice, begin with Civil Rights. That is the middle. How can you fight for Civil Rights, when you don't have human rights? How can they let a small few terrorize other nations, kill their people and steal their natural resources without standing up?"

"They don't know," Marcus said.

"Come on, Marcus, the world sees it, but they do very little about it. Take Iraq, a nation smaller than one of the fifty states. Saddam Hussein a dictator that the US put in power in the late '70's to undermine and overthrow

Ayatollah Khomeini. And when Saddam began to act outside the arms of the US, they went after him on trumped up charges of genocide, when the US were his conspirators. They killed way more Iraqi people than Saddam ever did, and they call the Iraqi people terrorists for fighting for their lives and their land after the US invaded their soil. Sounds like a freedom fighter, not a terrorist, but the US people have done very little about it, until hundreds of thousands of innocent lives have been lost. Have the people forgotten the African holocaust, the modern day slave trade, the Jewish holocaust? What is going on with the people that we died trying to save?"

"They've forgotten, and worse," Martin said, "they don't care."

"Only because they don't understand?" Marcus said. "Look at Bo Jack. Look at the power that young man has, and doesn't even know it. We sent him back so he could see all the blood he has on his hands."

"I've always told you two, that the young rappers were going to head a new Civil Rights movement," Martin said.

"You mean human rights," Malcolm corrected.

"Excuse me, Human rights," Martin said. "The rappers are beginning to read. Grand Master Flash was revolutionary when he brought out the song *The Message*. That's when I knew a change was coming. I just didn't think it would take this long."

"Money has blinded the world. And as these rappers began making so much of it, they didn't care about the message, only the means to make more money," Marcus said. "But now we have a new breed. These rappers have suffered in poverty, been victims of police brutality, and have seen so much misery and injustice before they made it as rap artists. And a small few of them haven't forgotten where they came from. These are our new leaders. Krs-1, Jada Kiss, Mos Def, Dead Prez, Common, Kanye West, Talib Kweli, Q-tip, and my favorite, Nas, to name a few. They care more about the message than the money. They are reading and re-writing history through their lyrics. They are Generals in Father's army."

"Yes, but with all successful armies there needs to be a leader," Malcolm said.

Martin waved his hand across the glass table. "And now I think we've found him."

"Let's just pray that Bo Jack is the man that we think he is," Marcus said, looking down at the young rap star, on his knees praying.

"He has a long road ahead," Martin said, "As we all do."

"If we can just get Barack to see a little more," Marcus said.

"He sees, but he is a strategist. He's fighting on our side, but Like Oprah Winfrey he's fighting from the inside out. They are playing their roles for Father, exactly as He wants them to," Martin said.

Malcolm intervened. "Passive resistance. I understand that, and it may work, but it will take much longer and so many more will die than if a more aggressive stand were taken against injustice. Oprah, could easily be a Winnie Mandela, or Assata Shakur and Barack could easily be more militant if he or she was raised in an environment similar to the one I grew up in. And I'm not talking about poor. I'm referring to the hostile times and experiences I went through growing up, or shall I say growing down, until I went to jail and was taught what up was."

"Both of you are right, because you both came from my school of thought," Marcus said. "Malcolm you were a modern day Ishmael, and Martin you were Isaac."

"Okay, Abraham," Malcolm said.

"If only you two would have come together in life," Marcus said, ignoring Malcolm's snide.

"With the following Bo Jack has amassed, and the generals that are already spewing conscious lyrics in their rap songs, we have a real chance for the people to place our Father back at the head of everything," Malcolm said.

"They have to overcome the fear that theirs eyes see. Bo Jack and the others rappers have to show the people that they are living in a prison bubble. Slaves to the dollar bill. Slaves to an antebellum system that is designed to keep them deaf, dumb and blind," Martin said.

"That will be a very difficult, if not impossible task. Father has sent an enormous amount of natural disasters to the US over the last two decades. And they still haven't taken heed to His messages. He has outlined the future in the Bible, Torah, and the Quran. The church has become such an entertainment sideshow and cashcow that the people blindly follow their spiritual leaders instead of following Father's messages that are in the Bible." Marcus pointed a finger in the air. "Not the words that man has so conveniently written in the Bible, but Father's messages between man's misleading words."

"The rappers are closer to Father than any bishop, pastor, Imam, or rabbi. These rappers are reading history. That is Father's word, as much as the Bible, Quran, or Torah is, even moreso in cases, depending on the history that is being read. After reading history, these young men are changing the way others think with their lyrics. They are the true Bishops, Imams and rabbis," Malcolm said.

"I agree," Martin interjected. "But, the black leaders and clergy will be their hardest fight, as it was mine, when Dr. Vernon Johns threw me into the fire at the onset of the Civil Rights movement. I just pray that Bo Jack will start a God-conscious fad as he has with the jewelry, and the clothes. If he can get people to understand what they are fighting for? If he can just get the people to see that my words still rang true today."

"And which words would you be referring to?" Marcus asked.

"An injustice anywhere is a threat to justice everywhere. The Middle East, Darfur, Jenna Louisiana, anywhere."

"First they have to be willing to die for freedom, and understand that as long as one person is wrongly persecuted by a system of injustice then no one is free from that tyrannical system," Malcolm added. "Look at Michael Vick. What he did was wrong, but what he has suffered far outweighs his acts. But people are scared to speak out. And the ones who aren't afraid, just don't care. Of course there are so many larger examples of gross injustices, Mumia Abu Jamal, Assata Shakur, Michael Bell, Troy Davis…"

"Okay, we get the picture," Marcus interrupted.

"Bo Jack has to get people to quit looking for Father in a man. The young man has to bridge the gap between Muslim, Christian and Jew. Get them to look at the sameness instead of the physical differences. Get them to see that Father is not relegated to one name. He is all and any name you use. He takes all calls, even wrong numbers." Martin shook his head, "It doesn't say for lack of reading the bible my people shall perish. The Bible reads, for lack of knowledge, and these young rappers or hungry for brain food, and however small, rappers like Common and Mos Def are making a positive impact just as the gangster rappers are making a negative one."

"As I've always said," Malcolm interrupted, "if you are not willing to die for freedom, then put the word out of your vocabulary. I think our friend here," they all looked down at Bo Jack, "is willing to die for freedom. It took him going back a few hundred years, but I believe he is ready to go forward," Malcolm said looking down at the young man, naked and on his knees with his head bowed.

THE MESSAGE

SELF-REFLECTION

1. Who is Mumia Abu Jamal?

2. Who was Marcus Garvey and what was the U.N.I.A. about?

3. Who is Geronimo Pratt?

4. Who was El Haj Malik El Shabazz?

5. Who is Dr. Maulena Karenga?

6. Who was Dr. Martin Luther King Jr.?

7. Which of these Great Kings do you most identify with?

Chapter X

Conversation with a Black Man

Only God can Judge me now.
Perhaps I was blind to the fact
I've been trapped since birth

-Tupac Shakur

"The Message*, 16 Life Lessons for the Hip Hop Generation* is an amazing book, but not nearly as amazing as its' author," the host said crossing her legs, holding the book in the air for all to see.

"Thank you, Queen, but I'm not nearly as amazing as the men who inspired me to begin writing, fifteen years ago, back in 1995."

"Tell us more about these men?" she asked.

"Well, I have to go back a little further in time so you can get a picture of the type of person I was, before these men saved me from myself."

She nodded her approval.

"Well, Queen, as long as I can remember, I've been one-hundred percent driven by the dollar bill. I remember watching as a friend's older sister took three packs of steaks, walked down a grocery aisle and put 'em down her pants, while her large T-shirt hung loosely on the outside. So, next I walked over to the meat section and checked the price on those steaks. My eyes got wide. I couldn't believe that two steaks had cost so much, around twenty-one dollars is what three packs cost altogether. Street price, ten dollars, I figured. Ten dollars was a lot of money for an eight year old, back in the '70's. And that's when I began my life of crime, steak stealing and selling to the candy lady in the projects."

"I read your semi-autobiography *Streetlife,* and I thought the part about how you began selling candy was hilarious." She smiled as she crossed her legs. "Would you mind sharing with our viewing audience the story of how you got into the candy selling business?"

"I don't know, but I guess I was around twelve or thirteen, it was winter. My only coat was an old blue nylon bomber jacket with more holes in it than a Connect Four game. I remember hiding some of everything and anything in the inside lining of that coat. One day I came up with one of my many ingenious ideas. I walked a couple miles to the nearest grocery store, A&P, went inside, walked to the candy aisle, looked left, then right, when I didn't see anyone or a camera, I began stuffing packages of snicker candy bars and packs of Charm pop, lollipops were the inside cotton coat lining should have been. After doing that a couple times, taking the candy to school and selling it before the homeroom bell rang, I decided to start catching the city bus around to Kroger, Big Star, Piggly Wiggly and others. I even came up with the genius idea to purchase some small item like a ten cent pack of Now& Laters while I had several packs of candy bars and blow pops concealed inside my coat, as to draw less attention to myself, coming in the stores every weekday."

She frowned. "You weren't scared of getting caught?"

"No, back then, I thought I was smarter than everyone else. I graduated from one hustle to another. Before I was old enough to drive, I paid car thieves to steal I-Roc Z-28's, Firebirds, and Trans-Ams. I'd then pay crackhead mechanics to strip the cars, taking seats, radios, wheels, and sometimes even engines out. Then I'd keep the parts in one of the crackhead mechanic's backyards, until I could find someone to load the parts up and take them to a junkyard, where I would sell everything."

"You never got caught?" she asked.

"Some of the guys who stole the cars did, but I never did. I always served as the lookout, whether it be stealing cars, or the stripping process. But, I did catch a couple theft by receiving charges later on down the line."

"Obviously, that didn't deter you?"

"No. Not really. I never served real time as a juvenile. When I would get caught, I'd always end up getting probation, or community service, a slap on the wrists as far as I was concerned."

"How did you get involved with drugs?" she asked.

"It began the summer of 1984. I was fifteen, never smoked or messed with any type of drugs. My father had just passed away in June that year. You would have thought he was the King of Indiana, bike riders from as far south as Tennessee showed and road at his funeral. I was awed by the hundreds of faces that sat and stood at my father's funeral. After the funeral and going back to Atlanta I started feeling alone, and I always wanted to be the center of attention, and the way to be that is to have money I figured, so for about a year off and on I would reflect back to how my father made his money, and I saw how many people loved him, even his five former wives that showed up to mourn at his funeral. He wasn't rich. He wasn't even well-off, but he was respected by all, and that's what I wanted."

"So, your father was the driving force behind your decision to begin selling drugs?" she asked.

He shook his head. "No, Queen. My perception of success, my perception of a black man's reality and worth was what made me start selling drugs. The only thing that stopped me in the beginning was money. Too many close calls in the car theft business, along with my name being implicated with the police more than once, made me decide to get out of that racket. After my father died, I sort of went into a money-making hiatus depression. It was one of the rare times that I had no money, when I decided the drug game would be my new hustle."

"Never one to start at the bottom, I wasn't about to stand on any corners, running up to cars selling dope. I was above that. So I convinced two other small time hoods that were older than me, to help me rob some small time drug dealers on other sides of town. It wasn't long before I saved up a little over five grand. That's when I got into the drug game."

"Reading your bio, and talking with you now, it seems you would have quit selling drugs after you almost lost your life and were paralyzed in the car accident, or heck even after you almost died in a holding cell after your first drug arrest," she said.

"Queen, you're speaking as if I were a rational person. Yes, I was intelligent as far as the streets were concerned, but without understanding of who you are and why you are who you are than there can be no rational. The only rational I cared about was how to get more money, more power, and more respect. And don't forget I was smarter than everyone else, so the arrests, the car accident, even the above ninety-percent chance that I would never walk again, were just freaks of nature, mishaps that had nothing to do with the destructive life I was leading."

"I truly was the king of fools, but didn't realize it until about a year after I began serving an eighty-eight month federal prison sentence for drug and gun charges. It was in prison that I met the most intelligent, articulate men, who happened to be black men. I'd never heard anyone speak so eloquently and passionately about the *'ignorance pandemic'* that has plagued Black and White America since before there was an America. I had never heard anyone speak of the heritage and the culture of African and African-Americans so proud and with so much passion. I was captivated as many cons were. I knew then that if I could speak like these brothas, than I could rule the world when I got out. If I could speak like them then I could convince anyone to slave for me as I came up with another scheme that wouldn't carry as much time as a drug offender."

"You mean to tell me," she paused, "that you were already planning a way to commit other crimes when you finished serving your time?"

"Queen, in my mind's eye back then, the only way a man like me could rise is through the back door, illegally. Back in the late twenties, early thirties, the father of Black History, Carter G. Woodson said, that *'we've been going to the back door for so long, no longer do we have to be told to go to the back door, we automatically go, and when there is no back door we cut one out.'* It is this backdoor mentally that I had that so many of our young and old black men have today. That is why I dedicated my life when I was in prison to try and resurrect the black man and woman into being the Kings and Queens that we once were, and still are."

THE MESSAGE

"If THE MESSAGE," she held the book in the air, "is any indication of how you are trying to achieve the goal of awareness, I'd say you are doing a very good and needed job." She applauded followed by a standing ovation and applause by the majority white female audience in the studio.

"Jihad Uhuru," Bo Jack whispered, his eyes still closed.

Brandi jumped up from her seat and turned away from the "Oprah Winfrey Show." "Girl you heard that?"

"Heard what?" Demetria said, removing the headphones from her ears.

Brandi pointed to Bo Jack Jones, the father of her only child, who looked to be sleeping peacefully in the hospital bed in his private room. "He just talked."

"You sure?" Demetria asked. "He looks the same as he has for the last three months, she said, leaning in over his hospital bed. Demetria was close enough to kiss him when his eyes popped open.

"Boo," he whispered, scaring Demetria so bad she rose up and fell into the machine he was hooked up to, knocking it over and pulling out the two IV's Bo Jack had in his wrist and arm.

"Boy, I oughta kill yo' ass," Demetria said, as Brandi helped her up.

"Girl, he's awake! He's awake!" His other babymomma, Brandi shouted.

"He's awake?" Demetria asked as she got to her feet. "He's awake!" she, too, shouted, realizing that Bo Jack Jones was indeed back among the living.

"Oh my, God! He's bleeding," Demetria said, looking at his arm, where'd she ripped out his IV's, instinctively, both girls looked toward his groin before sighing relief after seeing that his catheter was still hooked up.

"Bo, can you hear me?" Brandi asked, speaking loudly into his ear, while Demetria ran out of the room and down the hall to get help.

"Stop yelling, girl, and please get outta my ear, I can smell your breath through my ears," he whispered.

"In a coma for three months, and you wake up crackin' the same lame jokes." She put a hand on each hip. "Damn, I had so many plans. I was gon' use the life insurance money on making a movie about your life. You was gon' be bigger than Elvis. Usher, my future Baby daddy was gon' play the part of you." She threw her hands in the air. "Now you done woke up and ruined all my plans."

"Now you got jokes," he whispered with a smile on his face.

Doctors and nurses rushed in, ushering Brandi out of the room. Brenda Ellard, Bo Jack's mother, Demetria, and Brandi waited in the private emergency waiting room that was specifically set up for them, two doors down from Bo Jack.

A couple hours had passed before the head physician in charge of Bo Jack's care walked into the makeshift, private hospital waiting room.

Brenda grabbed the doctor's arms before he could get inside the room good. "Is my baby all right?"

"Your son is fine," he smiled. "Miraculously fine. We ran several tests, and I've never seen anything quite like this."

"Like what?" Brandi asked.

The doctor scratched the back of his head. "It's mindboggling. Ninety-days in a coma, incapacitated and his brain activity is absolutely normal. His nervous system is normal, and," the doctor looked at the chart he held, just to make sure for the tenth time, that he had read the test results properly, "he no longer has a heart murmur." The doctor shook his head. "I can't explain it, maybe in a couple days when his blood work comes back it will show something that will help us understand how his heart is stronger than it ever was." The doctor grabbed Brenda's hands. "Your son is supposed to be dead."

"No, Doc, God, don't make mistakes. My son is supposed to be doing just what he is. Living," she said.

The three women walked into the recovery room.

"Mom, Demetria, Brenda," he said sitting up in bed. "Demetria, Brenda, you are my closest friends and the mothers of my sons. We have a crazy friendship, but I thank God that it is what it is."

The three women in the room, especially Bo Jack's mother looked more shocked at his mentioning of God, than they were at him sitting up and speaking so clearly.

"I couldn't open my eyes, but I listened as Oprah interviewed and praised that brotha on TV," Bo Jack said.

"Jihad," Demetria said. "He been writing books for years. It's about time he got his props. *Preacherman Blues, Streetlife, Riding Rhythm, Baby Girl, MVP*, *Wild Cherry, Preacherman Blues II, MVP Reloaded, and that new World War Gangster*." She counted on her fingers. "Jihad's my favorite author. His books are so good, I can't believe it took Oprah this long to recognize him."

"His books are good, especially that *Preacherman Blues* and *World War Gangster*," Brandi interrupted. Kwan is my favorite, but Jihad is a close second," she said.

"Why haven't I heard of Jihad?" Bo Jack asked.

"You don't read," Brandi said.

"I haven't heard of him either, and you girls know how much I read," Brenda countered.

"I don't know?" Brandi shrugged her shoulders. "He isn't super popular, at least not until his latest book. All the others I had to order from Amazon.com, and from his website, jihadwrites.com, cause for some reason I can't always find him at Borders and I never see his books at Barnes and Noble."

"Girl, his books are on every corner in New York. Every time I go up there to shop, I make sure I check the book vendors for the latest Jihad book," Demetria added.

"Look," Brenda pointed, looking at the flat panel TV that hung from a pole connected to the ceiling a few feet away from the bed.

"You just came out of the coma. I can't believe the news media already knows," Brenda said watching the special report teletype going across the screen.

"Before I speak to any reporter or anyone outside of this room, I want to speak with this guy, Jihad," Bo Jack said. "Brandi, pay him whatever he wants, I need a month of his time."

"A month! What for?" Demetria asked.

"It's a surprise. Ladies, I am about to shock the nation and change the world," he said, not knowing how he was going to do what he'd just pledged.

*****

A week later, Bo Jack was rehabilitating his mind and his body at a private retreat in Dubai.

"Jihad, I'm sorry about everything being so rushed, and I know this was a weird request, but I need a brotha from the streets like you to teach me everything about my people, from the beginning to the end, in world record time," Bo Jack said as the two men took a seat at the bar overlooking the pool table that was in the suite.

"Little brother, I appreciate everything, the first class flight from the states to the fifty-thousand dollar retainer you paid me for a month of my time," Jihad said. "But, it would take me years to teach you everything I know about our people, and I'm still learning more every day."

"I understand that, bruh, but I will do whatever, for however long. I'll study and listen for eighteen hours a day, only taking time out to sleep, eat, and oh yeah," he pointed to an elaborate gym, surrounded by sound proofed glass walls, "and hit the gym."

"I'll do the best I can," Jihad said.

"That's all I ask."

"How soon you wanna begin?" Jihad asked.

"Yesterday," he replied. "But, I know you tired from the flight so tomorrow..."

Jihad stuck an arm out. "King, I'm on your dime now. We only have a month." He stood up. "Let me put my things away, take a shower and I'll be right back down. But, for now I want you to begin reading this book," he said, reaching inside one of his bags and pulling out *The Browder Files* by Tony Browder.

Thirty minutes later, Jihad walked down the piano key-colored spiral glass staircase. Bo Jack sat on the lounge chair reading while a massage therapist worked on his feet.

"How you doin', King?" Jihad asked.

"This is some powerful stuff," he said, looking up from the pages. "You must think I'm crazy."

"What do you mean?"

"My dream. Bringing you out here." He shrugged. "You know, just the whole idea of what I'm trying to do."

"King," he sat on the plush brown leather recliner across from Bo Jack, "I think you're sane and the world is crazy. What you've been through is not as unusual as you think." Jihad shook his head. "Unexplainable maybe, but not unusual. Since the beginning of time others have claimed to have out of body experiences, going back and forward in time. What you been through is sort of like a reverse prophesy, for lack of a better word, a miracle. To God, it's just another day at the office."

"So you believe me? You think my dream is real?"

"Very real." He nodded. "Your dreams are one of the few realities that exist."

Bo Jack tipped the massage therapist, and waved her away.

"The only reality is the unseen. These walls," he made an arc with his arm, "the mortar, brick, glass, everything you see changes. Reality does not. Reality is, was, and always will be. Take your body, any human body. A hundred years ago there was no Bo Jack Jones in the flesh, and a hundred years later there will not be a Bo Jack Jones, in the flesh. But your soul, king," he put his palm over his chest, "it has always been and will always be. And you can't see it. God is real. Love is real. The message behind your dreams are real. Evil is real. None of them change. They have always existed and will always exist, and you can't see any of them with the physical eye."

"Wow." He nodded. "Wow. Man, that's heavy." Bo Jack nodded. "Bruh, I've only read the introduction and the first two chapters of *The Browder Files*, and my mind is blown. In the introduction, Professor Hilliard broke down the ten steps to disorientating a people. I never thought a name was so powerful, but after reading the introduction, I understand why letting our names go is the first step."

"It's so simple, yet so sad, that we choose names for our children that sounds good to our ears. But we don't understand that the names sound good because someone that never wanted us to be free, systematically physically and mentally tortured us until we believed the things he beat into us. The name thing is so big, not only because it is the first thing used to identify you, but it gives the name bearer purpose, that is if the name means something. Take your name Bo. It's derived from Beauregard. A southern name of a white slave holder. What does it mean?"

Bo Jack shrugged.

"Nothing. So when your name is called, nothing comes to mind. But, take for instance my name. Jihad."

"Holy war," Bo Jack interrupted.

"No, but I'm glad you said that. It shows the noose that the news media has around your neck and the necks of most people, black, white, yellow and brown in this country. They are feeding you ignorance and we accept it, because we don't question what they say. Jihad means striving and struggling to bring others into the awareness of the oneness of God. In short, the word means *struggle*."

"I never heard that," Bo Jack said.

"I know." Jihad smiled. "Most people haven't. Why? Because they don't read anything other than what the media gets behind, or they only read novels. War is big money. Peace is not. So the war machine feeds false propaganda to the minds of the masses to manipulate the people into anger, and fear, which equivocates into money, big money. Jihad is a holy war, but holy war is not what Jihad means. Take for instance the word *revolution*. When Black kings and queens held up their fists in solidarity in the '60's and '70's, chanting and shouting *revolution*, the warmongers told America, that these were militant blacks, communists, terrorists. But what they meant was change, turn around, that's what the word revolution means. But it too is a war as well." He paused to let his words set in. "You follow me, King?"

"I'm there, at least I think I am."

They talked, Bo Jack took notes, and the two men read for hours, into the wee hours of morning.

Jihad looked at his watch, "Bo, I have to get some sleep before I fall out." Jihad rose from his chair and stretched.

"It's all good, bruh. I'm going to finish this book, take a few more notes before I turn in," he said, holding the book *Visions for Black Men* by Dr. Na'im Akbar. "This book has opened my eyes to so much. Nobody must be reading Dr. Akbar's work."

"Why do you say that?" Jihad asked.

"How can any man read this," he held up the red, green and black book, "and not do anything about what the school system is not teaching us?"

"People are reading, but like you, many feel passionate about Dr. Akbar's words, and the words of so many other pre-eminent African and African American scholars, but they also feel helpless in changing the mindset of people. You go try and explain a problem to a close friend outlined in say, Dr. Cornell West's book *Hope on a Tightrope*, see what type of response and what type of action your friend will take, or should I say, won't take to help solve the problem."

Bo jack jumped up. "But, we have to fight. We have to emancipate our minds. If we don't we'll continue the same cycle of slavery."

Jihad smiled. "I agree, but everyone doesn't have A.I.M. The attitude, the intensity and the mindset to fight for change."

"I do."

Jihad smiled. "I know you do, king. And we can continue this conversation in the A.M. Good night." He looked at his watch, "Or better yet, good morning."

Too exhausted to take the stairs to the third level of the suite, Jihad dragged himself to the suite's glass elevator doors.

*****

Three months later, two months longer than both men expected, Bo Jack had read, studied, and discussed thirty books.

"King, the only reason, I'm letting you go is because you won't let me pay you for the last two months," Bo Jack said as he embraced Jihad.

"You forgot the performance and all the awards you are sure to receive at the American music awards next month."

Bo Jack smiled. "You are going to be there with me and my crew, right?" Bo Jack asked.

"I wouldn't miss it."

"Just wait, I got something in store for the whole world." He smiled. "In the words of LL Cool J, *don't call it a comeback, I been here for years*."

Books Bo Jack Jones read

The Browder Files: Tony Browder

Visions for Black Men: Dr. Na'im Akbar

Mis-education of the Negro: Dr. Carter G. Woodson

The Autobiography of Malcolm X: Alex Haley

From Babylon to Timbuktu: Rudolph Windsor

Valley of the Dry Bones: Rudolph Windsor

Countering the Conspiracy to Destroy our Black Boys Vol. 1-5: Dr. Jawanzaa Kunjufu

Last Man Standing: The Geronimo Pratt Story: Jack Olsen

The Art of War: Sun Tzu

Slavery, The African American Psychic Trauma: Sultan A. Latif and Naimah Latif

Africa, Mother of Western Civilization: Dr. Yosef A. A. ben-Jochannan

Assata: the autobiography of Assata Shakur: By Assata Shakur

The Unseen Hand: Ralph Epperson

Pawns in The Game: William Guy Carr

The Iceman Inheritance: Michael Bradley

Part of My Soul went with him: Winnie Mandela

Black robes, White Justice: Bruce Wright

Stolen Legacy: Dr. George James

Powernomics: Dr. Claude Anderson

The Light of Ancient Africa: Dr. Na'im Akbar

Power to the People: Dr. Huey P. Newton

Nile Valley Contribution to Civilization: Anthony Browder

Soledad Brother: George Jackson

The Souls of Black Folks: W.E.B. Dubois

Breaking the Chains of Psychological Slavery: Dr. Na'im Akbar

They Came before Columbus: Dr. Ivan Van Sertima

World's Great Men of Color, Volume I: Asia and Africa, and Historical Figures Before Christ, Including Aesop, Hannibal, Cleopatra, Zenobia, Askia the Great, and Many Others: J. A. Rogers and John Henrik Clarke

Christopher Columbus and The African Holocaust: Dr. John Henrik Clarke

Blood in my Eye: George Jackson

Metu Neter Vol. II: Ra Un Nefer Amen

SELF-REFLECTION

1. "Without understanding of who you are and why you are who you are than there can be no rational." What does this mean?

2. Define success?

3. Does Jihad's past in any way sound familiar? And if it does how so?

4. Have you been involved or seen something, that you dreamed in the past? And if so how did it affect you? What did you think?

5. How can reading about your history, your culture empower you?

THE MESSAGE

Chapter XI

The Legend of Bo Jack Jones

Touch what I never touched before
seen what I never seen before
woke up to see the sun sky high.

-Goodie Mob

"Y'all my family. We all go back a long way and you know how I roll." Bo Jack paused, trying to find the right words. "We all been through it. We done lost family and friends to the streets. We done took so much from the streets." He scanned the faces of his thirty-member entourage as they sat at the studio conference room roundtable. "It's time for us to give back. The Goon Squad is dead. Bo Jack Jones is dead. Everyone who stands with me at the end of the day will be down with the God Squad."

"*God Squad?* What type of kick you on, fam?" Blue, one of Bo Jack's oldest partners in crime wore a clown frown on his face.

"Kick? Baby boy, I ain't on no kick. This is real talk. We 'bout to change the game in ways the world ain't never seen."

"The game ain't broke. We getting' money, real money, doin' what we do," Blue shot back.

"True that. But, it ain't always about the cheddar," Bo Jack said. "Imposters and mad scientists been playin' with our minds for centuries."

"Speak English, baby," Little John, one of the others spoke out.

"I'm talkin' about the slave system that said it was okay for the mass slaughter, rape and theft of our people, our land, and our minds. The same slave system that we are a part of today. The same slave system that we goin' to war with."

"Come on, playa," Blue said. "That 'white man got his foot on our necks' bag is played out. We gotta move on. The slaves were freed almost a hundred fifty years ago. We gotta forget about yesterday and live for today," Blue said.

"How can we forget what we don't even know? We don't have a clue what happened yesterday. Only yesterday we know about is the Alice and Wonderland yesterday the media, and the school system trains us on. If we truly knew and understood the lessons of yesterday, we wouldn't be asking the man for a job. We'd be creating jobs. We wouldn't be out in these streets killin', stealin', and burning down our communities. We'd be building communities, and killin' and stealin' ignorance from the mindset of our people. We wouldn't be up in here." Bo Jack stood up and waved his arms. "I got twenty-two cars outside in my garages. I shell out a hundred grand a month for these five buildings and my home." He held his arms out. "And most of our folks don't see a hundred grand in two, three years."

"Try five years," another interrupted.

"So, what you sayin?" Blue asked.

"I'm sayin' everybody down with me, gotta give it up to God."

"How you mean?" Little John asked.

"I'm gon' foot the bill for a six-month mind makeover, for all who wanna continue rolling with me. It's gon' be a lotta work. Ten hour days, five days a week. You will be re-educated by some of the top African minds in the world today."

"Come on, Bo," Blue said. "why waste your paper on some nonsense, when we getting' real paper in this music game. We on top of the world. We don't wanna be in some classroom. That's for squares."

"That's exactly what the Powers-that-Be want you to think, Blue. If you ain't down, I'll respect that, and we'll part ways. But this ain't open for discussion. I'm bringin' in Dr. Julia Hare, Dr. Marimba Ani, Dr. Na'im Akbar, Dr. Henry Louis Gates Jr., Dr. Ivan Van Sertima, and Michael Bradley."

"I thought Michael Bradley was white," one of the thirty said.

Bo Jack smiled. "He is. Who better to help us understand the *man*, than one of his own scholars that delve into the reasons why they have oppressed all peoples of color around the world."

For the next six months, Bo Jack and the new God squad minus six of it's original members read, studied, tested, and tirelessly worked with the intellectual dream team, as Bo Jack referred to the six men and women that helped reshape all of their minds. The six months was a spiritual transformation or re-awakening for the seven man God Squad.

Although Bo Jack cancelled his performance at the Grammy's, and he hadn't been seen in a year now, his music was still selling like ice in the desert.

He'd flown in Jada Kiss, Mos Def, Krs-1, Rakim, Common, Talib Kweli, Q-tip, Dead Prez, Floetry, Jill Scott, Lauren Hill, Brandon McMichael, and Jennifer Hudson, to collaborate on the new double album *The Black Love Movement Vol. 1.* Each artist involved pledged to do follow up albums, Vol. II, III, and so on, under Bo Jack's, new Forever Free record label.

The 2011 release of the album was an overwhelming success. Bo Jack's new name King Black was very fitting. The album became more of a movement, inspiring kids all over the world to learn their culture, and be proud of their heritage. It also sparked debates in Congress and the Senate. Students, black and white all over, were setting their school history books on fire, showing up to school on Columbus Day, and picketing schools on other days such as May 19th Malcolm X's birthday, and September 22nd, the day the Emancipation Proclamation was signed. Black College students all over America began legally changing their names to ones with afrocentric meaning, as another of the albums songs suggested.

It was a new and improved movement, one like the civil rights movement, but this was a human rights movement that demanded a new constitution as another of the songs on the album suggested. The N word had been replaced in most circles with the word, love. Women were addressed all over as Queen, and young men King.

The new leaders were not standing behind a pulpit with a cross hanging from their necks. The media did everything to discredit the rappers, and hip-hop and R&B artists, that led this new revolution.

THE MESSAGE

Playstation 3, 4, and 5, were being replaced by E-readers, Kindles, and books. The coolest guy in class was now the one who asked the most thought provoking questions, or had the most thought provoking answers.

Bo Jack Jones had long ago shed his slave name and had taken on the name King Black, which was fitting for the 1st album and the movement the album started.

The Black Love Movement is real, and it is coming to a city and school near you.

Forever Free Fam

King Black and the God Squad

SELF-REFLECTION

1. Can you see a movement like this every really happening?

2. Why do you think there is a Christopher Columbus Day?

3. Why do you think Black and Hispanic-American history is so non-inclusive in our school history textbooks?

4. What do you think the father of Black history; Carter G. Woodson meant when he said, "We have to first be willing to unlearn what we've been taught in order to break the chains?"

5. In the previous chapter, six African-American historians were brought in to teach King Black's crew, the God Squad. None of them were church pastors, but after the six months, the author spoke of how they had gone through a spiritual transformation. How could that be, when they were studying history, and the psychology of race and not the Bible, Koran, or Torah?

Chapter XII

Snitch Politics

I know where I'm going and I know the truth, and I don't have to be what you want me to be. I'm free to be what I want.

-Muhammad Ali

"Boy, you gotta be dumber than a bag of bricks. I mean, I'm dead serious," the old man said, lecturing his grandson.

"Why I gotta be all that?" Malik asked.

The old man placed both hands and put all his weight on the black metal cane while shaking his head from left to right. "You tell me."

"Just 'cause I ain't no snitch, I'm dumb now?"

Without warning the old man picked up his cane and swung.

"Grandpa?" Malik shouted, barely dodging the blow. "What's your problem?"

"You, and all the stop-snitching-idiots like you."

Malik wanted to get out of his grandpa's house before the old man worked himself into a coronary. He would've been gone, but he needed some gas money. Besides, since his mother cut him off after he dropped out of high school last semester he sure couldn't afford for his grandpa to do the same.

Malik sucked his teeth. "Grandpa, that's the problem. All these turncoat snitches. One time (the police) can't catch no one themselves, they rely on us to turn each other in." Malik shook his head. "Ain't no different than in the Pro-black movement of the 60's and 70's. They catch a brotha dirty and they offer him a free pass if he turns the next man in, or worse, they send him inside the Black party lines to be a spy, and report back to them so they can use the information the turncoat gave them to cause dissension in the parties. And don't get me started on how those Uncle Tom negroes snitched out runners during slave. . ."

"Stop right there." The old man held out his palm. "You new dummies got the game bass-akwards." He ambled over to the beat-up brown leather lounge chair in the small living room. "Boy, you gon' just stand there with your hands in your pockets or you gon' help me sit down?"

"Grandpa, I don't know why you don't get rid of that old beat-up thang," Malik said, helping his grandpa sit down in his favorite chair.

"Me and this chair done been through forty-years of history. And if I got any say so in the matter, we'll go through anotha forty." He waved at his seventeen-year-old grandson. "Now, you go on and sit down. I sees I gotsta put some knowledge in that ol' hat rack you got sittin' on top your neck."

"Grandpa, I gotta go. I ain't go no time to-"

"Ain't none of us got no time, but you act like you recyclin' time. Runnin' them streets doin' nothing, but goin' in circles. Now if you want some chump change from me, you best sit yo' narrow behind down and listen to what I has to say."

"How you know I need some money?"

"Didn't I tell you, you was runnin' around in circles? I watch you, boy, and you repeat the same ol' thing 'cause you don't understand. He pointed a long dark finger in the air. "You know better, but you don't understand."

Malik looked at his Timex before taking a seat on the new gray leather couch next to his grandfather.

"What if that little girl was your daughter, your sister?"

Malik shrugged his shoulders.

"What in hell does that mean?" He imitated his grandson's shrugging of the shoulders.

"I don't know?"

"Whachu mean you don't know?"

"What you want me to say, grandpa?"

"Something worth listening to. Because of this, this snitch code on the streets, you ain't gon' go to the station and tell who shot that baby."

"I done told you, I ain't no snitch," Malik said.

"Who, who you done told… Boy, as God as my witness, you talk to me in that tone one more 'gain, I'ma take my wooden leg off and cave yo' head in."

"Sorry, grandpa, but I ain't no snitch," he repeated.

"So, you a murderer now? 'Cause that's what you is, if you sit back and do nothin', while you sawed who shot that four-year-old girl. When them fools do anotha drive-by and kill someone's child, mother, or father that blood'll be on your hands, too."

"Just 'cause I won't go tell one time who did the shooting, I'ma murderer now?"

"Now, I know I stutter a little, but ain't nothin' wrong with my English."

"But, I'm sayin'…"

"I hear what you sayin' and it don't mean a hill of beans." He took his dentures out and put them in a cup on the stand next to his chair. "Back in slavery days, them negroes would do anything to move from the fields into the house. The snitchers, they was called the porch negro. They were the most dangerous of the slaves. They tell it, do it, and lie about it. Whatever it took to move from the fields into the house they did. That's what you was referrin' to. That was wrong. And back in the movement, the government, the local police, even the Klan used us against each other as you so pointed out. That, too, was wrong. But what you *new negroes* is doin,' is takin' us back to the 1700's. You *new negroes* done replaced the Klan and the slave master." He pointed a finger at Malik. "You killin' and destroyin' way more black folk than the Klan, the slavemaster, or the military could ever do. And anyone who let a crime go unreported is just as worse as the criminal."

"But, Grandpa…"

The glass fell on the floor as he reached for his teeth and flung them at Malik. "Boy, don't interrupt grown folk when they talkin'. Now, like I was sayin'. You killed that, little girl, and everyone else them fools gon' shoot, 'cause you ain't snitchin'. How you think that little girl's momma feel. What did that little girl do to deserve a hole in the head?"

"Grandpa, if I snitch then they gon' come after me. You want them to kill your grandson?"

"Hell, no, I don't, but if that happens, I will at least be proud in knowing that you stood for something, which validates your life. If you stood up, then maybe others will start standing up and this senseless murder, mayhem, and drug stuff will stop."

"Grandpa, you seventy-eight-years old, things don't work like they did when you were my age."

"Hell, if they don't. Only difference is, the killers that did the drive-bys, came wearing white sheets, and they had white faces. And they didn't live where we lived." He leaned forward. "Fifty some odd years ago, I was just like you, young, dumb, and full of myself. Now I was laid out in back of the juke joint when some of my boys got into a big fight with some ol' boys from across the tracks. 'Bout ten of em, maybe nine, minus myself, tore up Xenobia's Juke Joint in New Orleans that clear night. Now the po-lice knowed I wasn't in on the fightin', I was in a drunken stupor when they woke me up. But that didn't matter. They needed someone to answer to what had happened. Everybody at Xenobia's knew what happened, who was fighting, and who stabbed Jonny Ray Newsome to death. Just like they all knowed it tweren't me. But, I still did twelve years on the chain gang 'cause no one came forward, and I wouldn't tell who my boys were. And in them twelve years, I learnt a whole hell of a lot."

"Oh, I get it. 'Cause no one came forward in your case, and because you didn't go out like a snitch, you want me to come forward now?"

The old man looked up at the ceiling. "He favor me. Even got the Frazier nose, but Lawd God in Heaven, ain't no way in Sam hell this boy came from my loins," the old man said before turning his attention back to his grandson. "Boy, one ain't got a thing to do with the other. I'm just trying to show you that I lost twelve years of my life cause of a dumb ass code." He leaned forward. "Let me tell you somethin' and you can take this to the bank and cash it. One out of fifteen black men are in jail as we speak. And of those in jail, there are three types: those that snitched, those that wish they would have snitched, and those that didn't have nobody to snitch on. Is snitchin' right? At times it is, and at times it ain't. But, you have to use that thing on your neck for something more than a hat rack to figure when to speak and when to keep quiet. You have to do what is right, or wrong will follow you like a shadow until you start doing right."

Malik nodded, not knowing what to say.

"Them rappers singin' about being a balla, a playa, stop snitchin', but most of the ballas that retire from the game are snitches. Your major and biggest dope dealers, hustlers, pimps, murderers, all snitched. Y'all talk about loyalty in the game. What loyalty? They criminals, murderers, thieves. What thief is loyal? What murderer is loyal? Do you honestly think when Joe Blow gets popped with fifty kilos of that crack, he ain't gon' tell it to get a lighter sentence? You think Pretty Ricky gon' spend life behind bars, when he could just drop a name or two, sit on the witness stand, to get his Pretty Ricky life back?"

"I don't know."

The older man pointed. "Now see that's the problem, you don't know. That's why you ain't down at the police precinct becoming a hero. Now, if it was me, I'd take the police to them fool's houses and I'd knock on the door and point the shooter and everyone in the car out on national TV with a mile-wide smile on my face. Why? 'Cause I'll have made a difference. I would have got some of the evil off of our streets. And if they had a bullet with my name on it, it had my name on it before I told anyway."

*****

"I will never forget that day. Why didn't I listen?" Malik said, tears clouding his vision as he spoke at his four-year-old son's funeral. "That was ten years ago. Ten years ago. I witnessed a little girl get shot down almost exactly as little Malik. Like my Grandfather said, I might as well have pulled the trigger. And now I see why." Malik Mathew Frazier didn't even know who it was helping him to his seat. He'd been at the alter for the longest, crying and wishing he could turn back the hands of time. He couldn't get his son's angelic face out of his head. Only, it wasn't just his son he was seeing. He kept having visions of that little girl from ten years ago.

He'd seen that little girl on several occasions, but the one that haunted him now was the one of her with half her brains blown out the back of her head. And when he closed his eyes now, the only way he could picture his son, was of the way he looked lying in the blood stained grass with a mask of horror on his face and the cold stare of death in his eyes displayed as he held him six days ago in the front yard after the shooting.

Before the police even finished interviewing the twenty or so people that were playing throw-up football in the dirt field next door to Malik's house, he knew that no one would come forward with information, although someone had to get a good look at the vehicle and the shooter. It was the shadow that his grandfather had warned him about ten years ago, when he didn't come forward and tell who'd killed that little girl.

"What if it was your daughter, your mother, your father?" his grandfather had asked.

Malik sat in the front row, only a few feet away from his four-year-old son's casket.

SELF-REFLECTION

1. When is it all right to snitch?
2. When is it wrong to snitch and why?
3. Explain loyalty to the game? What is this, and how does it work?
4. If you were Malik, would you have gone to the police and told who the little girl's murderers were?
5. What did you learn from this story?

Chapter XIII

Definition of a Gangster

God and Nature first made us what we are, and then out of our own created genius, we make ourselves what we want to be. Follow always that great law. Let the sky and God be our limit and Eternity our measurement.

-Marcus Garvey

"You serious? You want me to blast shorty over a stack?"

"Am I smiling," Escobar said to his young soldier as they stood outside the Wing Joint across the street from the Thomasville Heights project housing apartments. The sun was at it's peak and as usual it was hell-hot this July day. The two men stood in back of what was once a Kroger grocery store.

"He been down with my crew since you turned it over to me two years ago," the young man explained. "I'll pay the gee out my money." He began reaching into his pocket. "His moms was short a thousand dollars, and without no insurance, J-J had to pay twenty stacks for her kidney transplant."

"That ain't your problem. That ain't my problem. He should have asked before he decided to take food out of my and your mouth," Escobar said. "I would let this pass, but this is the third time he done come up short since he been out on bond."

"Ohhhh," Baby C nodded, "I see what this is about now. You think J-J might talk to the folks?"

"Let me tell you somethin'. I'm thirty-six. I been selling dope longer than you been alive and I ain't never did more than six months in jail. Why you think that is?"

"'Cause you…" He shrugged his nineteen-year-old shoulders. "I don't know."

"Because I don't leave any loose ends. I watch what people say and I listen to their actions. Marinate on those words for a minute." Escobar paused while the young man nodded in thought. "I ain't never hired nobody to take a sucka out. I ain't never hesitated to put anybody six feet under. If you don't take heed to nothin' I say today, take heed to this," he pointed, "a dead man can't testify. Now your boy J-J been acting real funny since he been out on bond."

"Esco, you know J-J ain't no snitch."

"When them folks put that heat lamp on his ass, talkin' bout how much time he lookin' at, and how they gon' put the word out that he a snitch, if he don't give 'em something, that fool gon' go ta singin' like an R&B diva." The big man rubbed his beard. "The streets talk and what I'm hearing is your boy actin' real funny."

"Two months ago, back in May," he took a second to remember, "same day I posted his bond, his momma got sick and almost died," Baby C said, wiping sweat from his forehead. "How he suppose to act?"

The overweight drug kingpen ignored his cousin's question and asked one of his own. "You nervous about something?"

Baby C shrugged. "What I got to be nervous about?"

"You sweatin' like you nervous, like you holdin' somethin' back." Escobar crossed his massive arms and leaned against his snowflake white convertible Rolls.

"Esco, it's ninety degrees out here. I'm burnin' alive."

"Uhm-hm." Black Escobar said. "Let me find out you got some female up in you. I gave you the name Baby Capone, cause I thought you was gangsta. Was I mistaken?"

"Man, this me." He patted his chest. "Your baby cousin. You know how I get down."

"Your fight game and your knife game is nice, but it's time you start earning the title of a G. No excuses. It's time we dropped the baby from your name."

"Why J-J? He done paid me back the other times."

"'Cause you got feelings for the little punk. That's why." Escobar finger-jabbed his cousin in the chest. "Feelings is what gets a stunner busted. How you think Bundy, John Wayne Gacy and all of the famous serial killers got away with so many murders, and why you think serial killers like the Zodiac killer up in Frisco ain't never been caught?"

"'Cause they white," Baby C said.

Escobar reached out and slapped the young man upside his head. "Nah, fool. They were sociopaths. No feelings. That means no remorse for the cats they did in. And old Zodiac is still out there because he's careful, and he's not greedy. The reason I'm not in jail is because I ain't never left no evidence or witnesses. People respect my gangsta, and ain't no fool, fool enough to try and knock me from my square."

"But what about…?"

"What about what?" Escobar interrupted. "Ain't no ifs, ands, buts, or whats. You have to make an example out of the kid, so cats will know you bout it-bout it. All these fake ass gangsta wanna bes out here flexin' and saltin' the game. That's why all these snitches are runnin' around with ghetto passes. Cats is afraid to put some lead work in. Since you was a young'n, you wanted to be gangsta. All you listen to is that dirty south gangsta rap. You either gon' be a real G, or you might as well bend over, cause believe me, you gon' get tried, and one day you gon' get caught slippin' and somebody gon' put some heat up in ya."

"Why can't I cap him in the leg or arm? J-J's a good money maker," Baby C added.

Escobar grabbed his nineteen-year-old cousin by the neck, spun him around and threw him up against the rusted out grocery store dumpster."

The nine-millimeter burnt as it touched the back of Baby C's bald head. "I love you like a brother by a different mother." Escobar shook his head. "But love won't keep me out of prison. On everything I love, I will burn your black behind, right here. You represent me, Black Escobar, the King of the ATL. Hood legend. You my blood, and you gon' smoke that zero, or I'm gon' do you, him, and his no-kidney havin' mammy." He removed the gun from the back of his cousin's head. "Now, are you a real gangsta or are you a snowflake?"

The young man tried to keep his heart from jumping out of his chest. He blinked back the tears before slowly turning around. He took a deep breath. He couldn't show weakness. His big cousin was his idol. All his life he wanted to be a balla, a gangsta like his big cousin. The happiest day of his life was when Escobar introduced him to the thirty members of his drug dealing, thug family that answered directly to him. That was two-years ago, the day after he dropped out of high school to become a full time drug dealer. And that was the same day Escobar gave him the name Baby C. He'd never killed anyone, but he knew this day would come. If he didn't know anything else, he knew that the drug game was a cold, cut-throat game of survival by fire.

"All right." Baby C nodded. "I'll do the boy."

"Tonight."

"Tonight? I gotta plan it. I need a few days, at least. I gotta figure out how and where I'm gon' do it, and where I'm gon' dump the body."

"We just planned it. You watch too many movies. You ain't dumpin' nothin'. That's how you get caught. It's Wednesday. At four in the morning. Where you think he is?"

"Sleep, I guess."

"Don't guess, know. Where's J-J now?" Escobar asked.

"I guess he at the hospital," Baby C answered.

Escobar popped his cousin upside the head with an open palm. "Didn't I just tell you about guessin'. Guessin' instead of knowing is the quickest way to get you inside a body bag or a jail cell. Call the kid, find out where he at. Have him meet you somewhere as soon as you leave me. No phones. Tell him in person, you need for him to roll somewhere with you right now. Tell him to meet you somewhere dark and deserted. As soon as he gets within range, put one right here." Escobar pointed to his temple. "Do it quick, and use the silencer I gave you when I brought you in. Oh, yeah, and before you go home, drop the gun and the silencer in a sewer at least five miles away from where you smoke the kid."

"Where should I have him meet me?" Baby C asked, reluctance in his voice.

"Right here. We back here in broad daylight. Ain't no one came driving around this old abandoned Kroger. Easy in, easy out. You just make sure you get here first, and don't drive, park around the corner."

A couple minutes later, Escobar's Benz bent the curb, chrome dubs spinning and shining, as he pulled from behind the old abandoned Kroger. A Minute later, Baby C came out of the opposite end of the old store, his freshly painted, burnt, bright, sunkist orange Escalade burning the eyes of anyone who dared to look at the bright, sparkling SUV.

Little did he know that he was being watched.

*****

The moon had never been so bright, he thought as he waited for J-J. He wasn't a killer. He didn't know it until he was ordered to take one of his own crew out. He'd been sitting behind the dumpster since midnight. For almost four hours he'd sat in a ball crying and thinking. He wanted to be gangsta, but at what cost? He wanted people to look at him the way they looked at his cousin, but at what cost? He wanted the power that his cousin wielded, but at what cost? He could handle anything, and he could probably kill if backed into a corner, but kill for no reason? He didn't know if he could do that.

He stood up, shaking his head. He couldn't do it. He walked from behind the dumpster, when the whole area lit up. Headlights were slowly approaching. Baby C put the nine down the small of his back. Thank God he'd worn pants that weren't saggin, he thought as he began to walk toward the car.

"What it do, Baby C?" J-J asked getting out of his tricked-out gold Chevy Impala.

J-J was right in front of him. He'd been nothing but a friend to the young man the two years they'd known each other. And then, the words popped into his head: *You gon' smoke the zero, or I'll do you, him and his no-kidney havin' mammy.*

He never saw it coming. The gun bucked in his hand. Just like Escobar ordered, he put a bullet in J-J's head. The young black man slowly crumbled to the ground, his lifeless eyes fixed on his friend - his killer.

Baby C thought he was going to throw up, but he knew better. *Evidence,* he thought as he swallowed, refusing to soil the crime scene. He readied to run when the entire abandoned area lit up like an exploding bomb.

"Don't move!" a voice shouted from the loudest bullhorn, he'd ever heard. "Put your hands up! Now!" the voice barked. The lights came closer. He heard the whirring sound of propellers. He didn't have to look. He knew it was a helicopter. Just like he knew it was over for him.

*****

"Good work, Franklin. We should be able to turn this bust into at least four more," the man spoke into the receiver.

"That kid is soft. He know a lot of players in the game. Now that his mother's sick, and he's looking at life for murder and drugs, he should be ready to come on in and give up some other players in the game," Franklin spoke into the receiver. "How we gon' work it this time?"

"I'm sorry. I don't follow you."

"My dope. You know what I pay for a kilo of heroine. I know the department ain't gon' give me a hundred grand."

"Don't we always take care of you? You know it'll take a minute, but we'll get the kilo back to you."

"Last time it took a year," Franklin complained.

"All that money we letting you make. Stop crying. You sound like your cousin when we were listening to you two earlier. Just relax, Mr. Gangsta. Oh, and that story about the serial killers, loved it. Have you considered coming in and training our field agents how to be street level drug dealers?" the man asked.

"Captain, I done told you and I done told the director of the FBI himself that you can't teach this. You have to be born into the game to be a gangsta like myself. Besides, if I gave up the game, I'd be out the game. As long as I plant dope and set fools up for you, I'm free to do what I do best," James Franklin, also known as Black Escobar said before hanging up the phone as he pulled up to his aunt's house. He sat in the car a minute, trying to clear his head so he could get into character.

He squeezed his eyes together before pulling the bottle of Visine out of his pocket. This was the first time he'd had to break the news to anyone that their child was dead. Baby C was his first cousin, so he knew he had to cry. Just like he knew he had to set J-J up with a drug and murder beef, like he'd been ordered to do.

Escobar still couldn't believe how stupid his people were. He'd been running around shooting people like he was back in the Wild West. As he'd said, he'd never done any real time. The six months he served seventeen years ago was more than enough time for him to know that he couldn't go back. When the Feds first came to him with the deal, he was reluctant, but at his attorney's prodding, and looking at a life sentence for twenty-thousand dollars worth of crack cocaine, he decided that he'd rather be free and dodge bullets on the street than lose the lifestyle he so enjoyed. He never thought he'd end up being a lifelong confidential informant. He also never thought the feds were so dirty, giving him a free pass to buy and sell dope, keepin' it strictly gangsta.

*****

Twenty-five years later, Baby C, now Abdul Muhammed, stood at the front of the room teaching class. G-A-N-G-S-T-A, he wrote on the chalkboard. He turned and looked at his students. "By a show of hands, how many of you consider yourself gangsta?" he asked.

Every hand in the room shot up.

"Okay." He nodded. "Put your hands down." He crossed his arms and put a hand to his chin. He took a couple steps forward before letting his arms fall to his side. "O-G. Original gangsta. B-G, Baby gangsta." Abdul's head dropped to the grey concrete floor. "I killed a man when I was eighteen." The teacher shook his head from left to right. "The man who I grew up idolizing, the man who I sold drugs for, the man that gave me twenty-thousand dollars so my mother could get a kidney transplant asked me to kill his nineteen-year-old cousin, who had done nothing to me, and who was a good friend and my immediate superior. I," he stuck his left arm out, and closed one eye. "Pow, blew that kids brains through the back of his head. Why? Because my idol told me that puttin' a body under my belt would put me on G status. Straight gangsta, Black Escobar had told me."

Abdul sat on the corner of the teacher's desk, and stared into the faces and eyes of thirty black men from the age of eighteen, to fifty. "I'm in here teaching GED classes while serving life behind bars cause I wanted to be gangsta. I was a fool and," he made a sweeping arc with his left arm,

"You're all fools for wanting to be something evil and twisted. I will never have kids. I will never leave these walls. And worse, that innocent boy's mother..." His words trailed off as he shook his head, tearing up.

The men dressed in prison browns sat in their chairs, their eyes glued to the most intelligent man that most of them had ever met, heard or seen.

"Anybody can squeeze a trigger. I can sell dope from a wheelchair. Anyone can manipulate the minds of a few lost souls, be it men or women." He stood and walked forward. "But to do what Dr. Ivan Van Sertima, Dr. Asa G. Hilliard, Dr. Maulena Karenga, Dr. Cornell West, and many other African-American scholars and historians are doing is what the true definition of gangsta is. Does anyone know who these men are, or what they're doing?"

Seconds turned into a minute, and one minute became two. No one raised their hand.

"These men. These kings are speaking truth to power. They are laying down a legacy of gangsta truths. These men are historians, scholars that went to school and dedicated their lives to exploding the myths that keep so many people of color ignorant. These men are standing up and speaking out against the system that is largely responsible for our twisted mindset. These men are fighting for all of our mental emancipation. They are writing books, lecturing, and teaching us where we came from, and who we were."

"If I had known then what I know now, because of these men and several others that are totally alien to our primary and secondary American school systems, I would've had pride knowing and understanding how my ancestors handled their business. We all hear about us coming from queens, and all the we-shall-overcome-struggle, but until you read the words for yourself, until you delve into the lives of people like Hannibal, Queen Catherine, King Solomon, Harriet Tubman, Malcolm X, Asa Phillip Randolph, Ida B. Wells Barnett, Assata Shakur, Geronimo Jigga Pratt and others you will be forever lost and confused." He shook his head with vigor. "Don't live another day not knowing. Don't die a fool. Pick up a book, any book by any of the above and start finding out why others don't want you to know who you are and where you came from."

SELF-REFLECTION

1. Go to your school library and ask your local librarian to order books by any of the African-American scholars, or books about the lives of any one of the heroes and sheroes that I named.

2. Do you really think there are drug dealers out on the streets that have a quote unquote free pass to commit crimes as long as they help law enforcement, trap and entrap others?

3. What can you do as one individual to deter someone from leading a gangsta lifestyle?

4. Why do you think so many young men are lured into the drug culture?

5. What does loyalty to the game mean, and do you honestly think that a man or woman selling drugs, killing people, robbing people, would respect a "no snitching" code when apprehended by law enforcement? They are already out there crossing people out, ruining and taking lives, now what would they be loyal to, and why would they hesitate to tell or even lie about someone else's illegal activities?

Chapter XIV

Sins of the Father

Black men born in the U.S. and fortunate enough to live past the age of eighteen are systematically conditioned to accept the inevitability of prison. For most of us, it simply looms as the next phase in a sequence of humiliation. Being born in a captive society and never experiencing any objective basis for expectation has the effects of preparing me for the progressively traumatic misfortunes that lead so many black men to the prison gate. I was prepared for prison. It required only minor psychic adjustment.

-George Jackson

"What in God's name?" Leroy's younger brother, John asked as he stared at his nephew's lifeless body laid out next to a Motel 6 vending machine. "What did you do?"

"I knocked his butt out," Leroy said, as he stood over his eighteen-year-old son.

"You said you was just comin' to get the boy," John said to his brother.

"I am. Help me get him to the truck," Leroy said, bending down and grabbing one of his son's arms.

John bent down and helped his brother get his groggy nephew up. Hookers, addicts and dealers watched as the two men carried the young boy down the motel stairs and to the black work truck.

It was Friday, August first, Mother's Day is what the hustlers called it. Not just Atlanta, but in hoods all around the country. Check cashing joints were standing room only. Welfare and social security checks came in the mail on the same day when the first fell on a Friday as it had done this particular one. This was also the day that more drugs were sold than any other time. It seemed as if the whole country got high on this particular day. Everybody but Leroy, John, and Leroy Jr.

"I can't believe you hit me," Leroy Jr. said, his hand caressing the left side of his face, while sitting in the middle of his Uncle's F-150 work truck.

"I can't believe you out here selling crack," his father said.

"Dude, I'm a grown man. You can't be handling me like this," the young man said to his father as his uncle drove in silence.

Leroy Sr. shook his head from left to right. "Dude? Boy, don't address me as dude. I'm your father, not one of your buddies or some street punk."

"Father? Is that what you call yourself? Been gone since before I could walk. Now, you been out three days, and all of a sudden you wanna play daddy?" Leroy Jr. shook his head. "Man, I'm grown. It's too late to play catch, dude," the young man said, pain in his voice.

"That's why I knocked yo' butt out in the first place. Call me dude or man again and you might not wake up the next time I lay my hands on you."

"What you want me to call you? Pops? Daddy? Man, I don't even know you," the young man said, still clutching the side of his face.

The words stung so hard, the elder Leroy had to blink back tears. Sitting right next to him was the reincarnation of himself. The slick mouth, the false bravado, even the swagger in his walk and talk. "I'm sorry for hitting you, Son. I'm sorry for so much, but there is a chance for you. There is a chance-"

"Chance! That's a joke. Only chance for me is the chance I make for myself. I came in this world by myself and I'm gon' leave this world by myself."

"What the hell does that mean?" Leroy Sr. asked.

"I'm just keepin' it real."

"You don't even know what real is. Real is the two out of three black men born in poverty going to prison. Real is the drugs and violence that has decimated urban communities all around this country. Real is all these rappers and video games glamorizing crime, and knuckleheads like you feeding right into the false hype. Real is our young sisters shakin' they tail and turnin' tricks for a dolla."

Leroy Jr. interrupted. "Don't forget the realness of fathers coming home from prison and actin' like they care after being gone for years, leaving brothas like me to embrace the streets. The streets fed me, clothed me, schooled me." He paused. "That's the only daddy I know."

"I see why he knocked your disrespectful behind out," John said. "Boy, whether you can see it, or believe it, your father loves you. If he didn't, he wouldn't have risked going back to prison coming up in that, that dope trap motel. He wouldn't have sent every dime home however little it was every month for the last eighteen years to help your mother with you. Show some respect."

Leroy Jr. turned to his left. "I'm sorry, Unc, it's just… You know it ain't no joke out here."

"Talk to your father. Tell him you sorry. He's the one that's trying to save you from yourself," John said, pulling up to a red light.

Leroy Jr. let out a deep sigh. "Sorry, LB," he said, addressing his father the way everyone had three nights ago at his father's coming home party. "You come up in my spot, on the biggest money making night of the year and start tripping on me getting' money the same way you did back in your day. And then, you embarrass me in front of my boys and the competition." He looked down at the truck's dirty floor. "I swear fo' God, if I coulda got to my nine…"

"You woulda' what?" His father interrupted. "You woulda shot me and you woulda' been in jail."

"Like father, like son," the young man interrupted, a ton of animosity in his voice.

"Look," his father began trying another tactic. "You right, I was never a father to you. I was in jail since you was a baby. Ain't nothin' I can say to take the hurt away. Ain't nothin' I can do to change the past. But I can do everything from preventing you from following in my footsteps. I love you."

"I can't tell. If you love someone, you don't leave them like you did me. You ain't gotta clue to who I am and what I been through," the young man's voice began to break.

"I think I do." Leroy Sr. nodded. "I was you. Your grandfather, my daddy…" He paused to reflect back in time. "I was with him the night he was gunned down by a rival number's runner in Cleveland. I was only five and your Uncle John was three. There were so many factors that drew us to the call of the streets, one being the lack of male guidance. The lack of our father being in our lives. And we both did time. Your Uncle did sixteen years and I did eighteen. Neither of us pulled the trigger on anyone, but both of us were guilty of murder all the same. A mother of three kids, babies, Od'ed on the heroine we sold. We didn't know the dope was bad." He paused. "I take that back, yes we did. All dope is bad, but this particular package took one of the fiends out sooner rather than later. Neither John nor I can ever give that woman's children their mother back. For eighteen years I've thought about that woman, her kids, what we did."

"The day after I got out, John told me you were out here slingin' dope. I cried like a baby." He held the back of his hands out toward his son. "John, turn the interior lights on." A second later, the inside of the truck lit up. "See these bruises and scars."

Leroy Jr. just stood straight ahead, not acknowledging his father's battered hands and knuckles.

"I got these from banging my fists on the concrete steps outside John's apartment after he told me what you were doing. If he wouldn't have grabbed me, I probably would've broken all the bones in my hands or…"

More worried about how his uncle knew what he'd been doing for the last few weeks, Leroy Jr. cut his fathers story short and turned to his uncle. "Unc, how did you know?"

"Beverly," John said.

"Momma? How she know? I ain't bought no clothes, no car. I'm always in the streets, so she …"

"Nephew, a mother knows when something ain't right with her children. Especially Beverly. She grew up in the hood. She done known me and your father since we was kids. Behind all the degrees, the Phd, she's still a mother and one who knows the street mentality. I don't know if she told you, but your father persuaded her to use the money we left behind when we went to prison to attend school. She wanted to put the money away for your college education, but your father balked, explaining that she had to get out the hood, better herself so she could provide a better life for you.

They pulled into a Quik Trip gas station. "Y'all want something from the store?" John asked getting out of the truck.

"I'm good," Leroy Jr. nodded.

"Get me a Diet Sunkist, bay bruh," Leroy Sr. said. "Where you goin'?" Leroy asked his son, as he slid over and out of the driver's side.

"Three six foot men in the front seat. I need to stretch my legs," he said before closing the driver's door.

Leroy Sr. got out on his side. "It sure is a beautiful night," he said looking up at the stars.

"It was a beautiful night, until you kidnapped me. No tellin' how much money I'm missing."

"You don't get it do you?" Leroy asked his son.

"What is there to get?"

"I'm trying to save your ignorant ass from ending up like me and your uncle."

"Psst. Help the bear. I don't need savin', except, from you," he said looking at his father across the truck's rear bed.

Leroy Sr. threw his hands in the air. "I…." he closed his eyes, balled and unballed his fists. "What do you want me to say. I'm sorry. I'm sorry, Leroy. I love you, never stopped and never will. You are my son. You are me when I was eighteen. And that scares me to death. I messed up half my life, you don't have to mess up yours. You can go to school. Get a job."

"Man, look. I done been the job route. Ain't nobody trying to hire me but McDonalds and Burger King and I don't work no five-dollar an hour gig."

"So, you'd rather be a twelve cent an hour flunky?" Leroy Sr. asked.

"Huh?"

"Twelve cents an hour, that's what you'll start out at in federal prison. After a year you might be up to nineteen cents an hour unless you go work for UNICOR, manufacturing everything from clothes to helicopter harnesses, stealing jobs from others in the free world. There you can make as much as a dollar and twenty cents and hour."

"I ain't you and Uncle John. I ain't trying to sell dope forever. Just 'til I come up and figure out my next move."

"So, you don't care about the people you hurting? The lives you helping destroy?"

"Dude, you think I'm the problem. Man, look around." He waved an arm in the air. "These stores, these people. Psst. Ain't Jack gon' change if I stop slingin'. The fiends still gon' get high, only thing is I won't benefit off they money."

"Keep calling me dude." Leroy Sr. nodded. "It's one thing for people to think you a fool, but it's a whole other thing to open your mouth and remove all doubt. And that's what you just did. Fool, you are the problem. I was the problem." He pointed to the double doors of the Quik Trip. "Your Uncle was the problem. It only takes one. One person to make a difference, as it only takes one person to take away someone's tomorrow. Every rock you sell that someone smokes, takes a little of their life away each time they take a pull."

"What about my life?" He banged his chest. "Don't nobody give a damn about me." He shook his head. "I done filled out application after application. Every time I go in a store or anywhere, when I ask if they hiring, I get looked at like I'm a disease before they give me that fake smile and say not right now, or hand me an application. But does anyone call me? Hell no."

"I wouldn't hire you either coming into my place of business with braids zig-zagging all up in your head and earrings on. If I was white, I'd be scared you gon' rob me. Hell, a black man, any man would be scared to hire you. Son, you want a job, you take a job or make a job."

"Take a Job?"

His father nodded. "Yes, take a job. Go on the web. Research the company you plan to go to. Study their products, research their founding date. Find out how they began, who founded the business, who is the CEO now, their last quarter or last years profits or deficit. Commit as much to memory as you can. Cut your hair, take them diamond studs out your ears, and cover up them tattoos. Pull some sample resumes up on line, use them to create your own resume, put on a suit and tie, pants on your waist and don't call, go to the establishment and look any and everyone in the eye and ask to speak to the GM or someone in HR. If the person you're speaking to asks why, tell them you're there to show them how to increase their profits from whatever they were when you looked them up."

"Man, that's a lot of work, and still ain't no guarantee Imo' get the job. What if they ain't hiring?"

"Anytime you can convince someone that you can increase their profits, and they like you, they will find a way to hire you. It's all about selling yourself. Be positive, assure them of how driven you are, how assertive you are and how you will go not just the extra mile, but the extra ten miles. And when asked what are your future goals, tell tem to own a company like theirs."

"I do all that, and what if I still don't get the job?"

"You move on to the next company. Don't matter if we're in a depression and there is a hiring freeze everywhere in the country, you wow the decision maker," Leroy Sr. pointed a finger across the bed of the truck at his son, "and they'll find a way to bring you in. Like I said son, bottom line, a business's number one priority is," his arms over the trucks bed, he rubbed three fingers together, "that dollar, and during hard times owners and managers are looking harder for people like yourself who can help the company make money."

John approached, his hand inside a plastic bag. "Look at me," John said, crunching on some flaming hot Cheetos. "Like you nephew, I ain't never been a five, four, or three dollar an hour brotha, well, that was until I went to prison. Then I had no choice in the matter. But, nevertheless, I had a plan for when I got out. I knew wasn't no one gon' give a thirty-seven-year old extra-crispy black, six-foot ex-con a job, so I sucked up my pride and took the job my probation officer helped me get after I got out."

"Unc., I still don't see how you mopped floors and cleaned Burger King bathrooms."

"I cleaned toilets in prison for five-dollars and twenty-five cents a month. That humbled me enough to not let my pride get in the way of me cleaning floors and toilets at Burger King. Those four months, I worked at BK, I endured stares, ridicule, and I was ashamed of having to work with a bunch of high school kids. But what kept me going was my ultimate goal. Owning my own business, and in four months with two thousand dollars in my pocket, that I had saved, I bought that '79 pick up."

Leroy Jr. smiled. "You paid for that thing. That rust bucket was the raggediest truck in the world."

"Maybe so, but it was mine." He smiled. "With that truck, a lawnmower, weedeater, a blower, and a couple gas cans, I went into business. I went door to door, asking how much they were willing to give me to cut their yard. I even cut, trimmed and landscaped yards for free to earn peoples business. Now, less than two years later I own three trucks and I have two crews working for me. They say it's a recession, no jobs, but that's because folks been raised and schooled to get a good job, instead of making a good job. Black people always depending on somebody else to provide them with a means to make a livin', with the exception of hustlers, and drug dealers." He put an arm around his nephew. "As long as the sun shines, grass is gon' grow. And as long as grass grows I, you and everyone else has a job."

"Never thought of it like that, Unc."

"Hell, I know you haven't," he said, before turning up the bottle.

"Hey, that's my Sunkist," Leroy Sr. said. "My bad, big bruh. Them Cheetos was burnin' a brotha's throat, I'll get you another," he said turning and walking back into the store.

"Leroy, son, I'll help you find your way, just give me a chance. I don't have all the answers. I don't even know all the questions, but we can both learn as we go. I've made enough mistakes for both of us. I just wanna be in your life. Your uncle was right. But we don't see the grass until it's taken away from us. We don't respect our freedom until we know that we no longer have it. The system is hard, especially for a black man, but the system is what it is until we change it. And the way to begin is changing ourselves from within. We have to be examples first. You're intelligent, Leroy. Hell, you got my genes." He smiled. "You just have to think, and then apply yourself. If you want more, than you have to do more. Make it happen. I want you to go to school, but more importantly I want you to do what you enjoy. Don't worry about the money, that'll come if you love what you doin', and if you love what you doin' it'll never be work."

Leroy walked around the truck with his hands in his pockets. "Okay. Okay." He nodded, before reaching out and embracing his dad. Unknowing to his father, while they held each other, Leroy Jr. unballed his left hand and threw the sandwich baggie filled with little crack rocks into the trash can. "Let's make a job together, dad."

A police car sped up the street, lights and sirens blaring. "You won't get this one," Leroy Sr. mouthed, shaking his head up and down in triumph.

SELF-REFLECTION

1. Right now, whether you are 15 or 55, what marketable skills do you have that will help you get hired, or successfully run your own company?

2. Name five jobs that you can create, with the skills you currently possess.

3. What are you doing now, to prepare for your future in the workplace?

4. Get a job, you are renting out your time, make a job, you own your time. What does this mean?

5. What is more important than making money?

Chapter XV

I Pledge Allegiance ...

You can only be destroyed by believing what the White world calls a ***Nigger.***

-James Baldwin

One dictionary defines the word nigger as "a disparaging term for a Black person." But we know different, right, black people? I mean a **nigga** is a good thang, right? It has to be, because we feel such a strong sense of pride when we lovingly reach out and address our peeps with 'What up, **nigga**," "My **nigga**," and my favorite, "I love that **nigga."**

Now, instead of trippin' off that word, we need to get over it and embrace a **nigga**. What we need to do is trip on that senseless holi-day.

After all, isn't January 15th, the stupidest holi-day. They should've named it **National Nigga Day**, instead of King day. National Nigga day, yeahhhhh. A day *where all my niggas get together to smoke blunts, drink 40's and party like it ain't no tomorrow. Martin Luther* ***WHO****. That nigga* *dead and forgotten. Everything he stood for don't mean Jack to a nigga now.* I mean let's look at history.

Black folks were stripped of their language, heritage, spiritual beliefs, culture, clothes, and dignity by the people who discovered the first nigga. I think that first nigga went by the name Boy, before the white man gave him the name that most of us have come to love, **NIGGER**, which we ebonically pimped out and changed to **NIGGA**.

Anyway, that history mess don't make a difference. Hell, we don't even pay no attention to it. What does make a difference is the state of Niggaism that my niggas who don't know they my niggas are in today. You know who I'm talkin' bout.

The **HATERS**, the ones that talk about Black pride, and the upliftment of Black folks, and they broke just like the rest of us, and they think they too good to smoke a blunt with a **nigga**. One of them same **Hater Niggas** just asked me where, **Niggaville**, **Nigga** Africa was. I told the fool wasn't no such thing. Just to show you how ignorant his suit and tie wearing ass was, he gon' tell me there had to be a **Niggaville** or a **Nigga, Africa** because like the names of the Chinese, Europeans, and the Americans yada-yada that identified where they were from, our name had to as well. Ain't that some crazy stuff, my **niggas?** The **Hater** even went on to say that the vast majority of people even gave their offspring cultural surnames after their ancestors.

Let me wrap this up 'cause that new B@#$%ch, Freak nasty's new video is about to premiere on BET, and I gotsta check the B@#$%ches out in her new video. Anyway, stop trippin off a **nigga**. We gon' keep gettin' high, and callin' ourselves **nigga**. We gon' stay ignant and freak B@#$%ches. Like one of the greatest niggas of all time Snoop Dog said, **"Ain't nothin' but a G thang, baby, 2 loc-ed out niggas**

goin' crazy" that's what's happenin', loc-ed out niggas goin' crazy over the word nigga. And NO WHITE MAN, you still can't use it. Why? 'Cause a **nigga** will kick a nigga ass and bust a cap in anotha **nigga** if you **Mr. White man** call me a **nigga.**

Holla,

Peace love and to all my **niggas** thuggin, and my niggas behind bars, I love y'all **niggas.**

Yours Truly,

Clarence Thomas Willie Lynch Washington AKA Uncle Tom

SELF-REFLECTION

1. Where is Niggaville, or Niggerland? If you are a nigga, then there must be a land named after you. What country do niggas come from?

2. Have you ever heard a Korean-American say to his Korean-American friend "What's up slant-eye?" Have you ever heard a White-American, say to his White-American friend, "What up my cracka'?" Have you ever heard a Native-American say to his friend "What up my Indian?" HAVE YOU EVER HEARD ANYONE OTHER THAN AFRICAN-AMERICANS lovingly denigrate each other as we do one another?

3. If the 'N' word is just a word and you don't mean any harm by using it, than why when we discuss it in a public forum do we call it the 'N' word, and why do *We* get mad when others besides *Us* use it.

4. Is it tradition, ignorance, brainwashing or all of the above the reason why *We* accept what the slave master told us that we were. Niggas, dogs, cats, fox's, etc.

5. Can you name anything positive that comes out of calling someone a nigga?

Chapter XVI

FREE YOUR MIND

When I discover who
I am, I'll be free.

-Ralph Ellison

Growing up in a world where the dope man was
King of the rejects
In the projects
And you were suspect and subject to his wrath
If you didn't give him his respect
And that's how I came to the realization
That my claim to fame
Was only as strong as my game,
And at the age of eight
I sealed my fate
Stealing everything from
SCHEMES to DREAMS
selling anything from
HOPE to COKE
Wore platinum before it was cool.

J. S. FREE

Little did I know
I was branding myself as a fool
Millionaireat 21
By 22, stick a fork in me
I was done
Locked up and locked in
A concrete, steel worldfull of what I thought
Were lost men.
No matter how crazy this may sound
Let me tell you what I found
Malcolm X and Martin King
Shootin' the breeze
Just hangin' around.
I asked how could this be?
Everybody knows you two are dead and gone
And suddenly Martin spoke the words
The POWERS THAT BE had led me and my
everybody wrong.
So, they handcuffed my mind
Took me on a journey through the pages, ages,
and stages of time.
I sighed
And cried
Not for my crimes
But the mind
And self that I never knew,
Or had a clue
To the trues that were in books
That I never read
Cause no one had ever said
Or led
Me to be fed
The untold facts

THE MESSAGE

The significance and beauty
Of being BLACK
And on track
To reclaim the freedom of being,
Believing and seeing
The GOD in me,
The God in you
As I
And we
Are meant to be
To be
FREE…. FREEE… FREE…
READ A BOOK
FREE YOUR MIND.

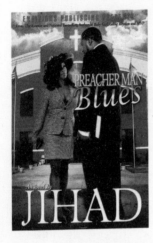

WILD CHERRY

By JIHAD

Cherry is one bad chick. That's no surprise since she's the granddaughter of one of the most thorough hitmen in history, Daddy

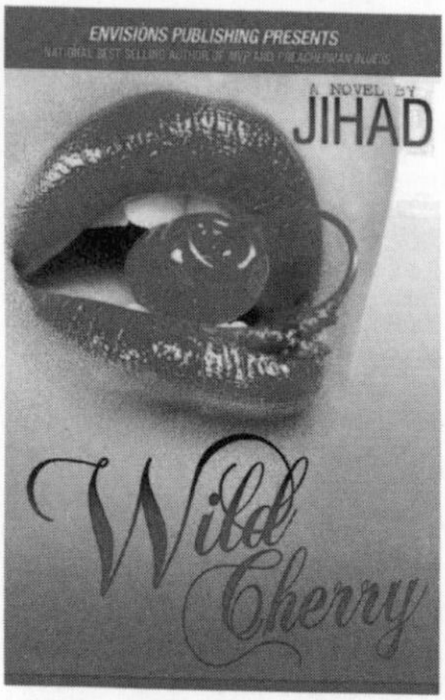

Cool. An NFL Superstar and bad boy himself, Jordan Hayes is about to find that out the hard way when he decides to make Cherry a pawn in his game of lust, drugs and lies. After Jordan moves on, he forgets all about the girl he once called "Wild Cherry." But Cherry hasn't forgotten about him. In fact, he's all she can think about as she does her time in a state mental institution. You play...you pay

Jordan's twin brother Jevon has been living

in his twin brother's shadow for years. When an encounter with a beautiful young lady opens the door for him to not just follow in Jordan's footsteps, but assume his whole identity, Jevon jumps at the chance. But Jevon is in for a rude awakening when he discovers the real reason his new woman is called "Wild Cherry."

ENVISIONS PUBLISHING, LLC

P.O. Box 83008, Conyers, GA 30013

Enclosed: $_____in check or money order form as payment in full for book(s) ordered. FREE shipping and handling. Allow 3-5 days for delivery.

ISBN 978-0-9706102-3-2 Wild Cherry $12.00

Name______________________________________

Address____________________________________

City___________________State_____Zip________

THE MESSAGE
BY J. S. FREE

The path from boys to men is paved with obstacles...with prison rates soaring, graduation rates dropping and the streets claiming a

growing number of young black men, only the strong can survive. Now, there's help to navigate the turbulent path to manhood. It's called The MESSAGE, an easy-to-read, inspirational, page-turning book, full of true- to-life short stories that creatively attack the heart of problems that so many young men of color face growing up in today's society. Not just stocked with problems, THE MESSAGE is filled with solutions. Each essay is designed to spark discussion to help young men make better decisions, motivate them to strive for more, and propel them to a lifetime of success.

ENVISIONS PUBLISHING, LLC
P.O. Box 83008, Conyers, GA 30013

Enclosed: $______________in check or money order form as payment in full for book(s) ordered. FREE shipping and handling. Allow 3-5 days for delivery.

ISBN 978-0-9706102-8-7 The Message $12.00

Name________________________________

Address________________________________

City____________________State_____Zip________

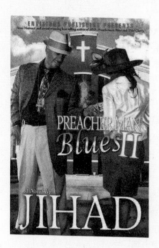

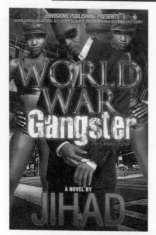